THE FUNNIEST SANTA CLAUS STORIES EVER TOLD

150 Real-Life Misadventures from a Professional Kris Kringle

KEVIN NEARY

Skyhorse Publishing

Skyhorse Publishing books may be purchased in bulk at special discounts for sales promotion, corporate gifts, fund-raising, or educational purposes. Special editions can also be created to specifications. For details, contact the Special Sales Department, Skyhorse Publishing, 307 West 36th Street, 11th Floor, New York, NY 10018 or info@skyhorsepublishing.com.

Skyhorse® and Skyhorse Publishing® are registered trademarks of Skyhorse Publishing, Inc.®, a Delaware corporation.

Visit our website at www.skyhorsepublishing.com.

10 9 8 7 6 5 4 3 2 1

Library of Congress Cataloging-in-Publication Data is available on file.

Interior illustrations by Andy Beauchamp, unless otherwise noted.

Cover design by David Ter-Avanesyan
Cover photo credit: Getty Images (Santa); Shutterstock (gingerbread)

ISBN: 978-1-5107-6607-5
Ebook ISBN: 978-1-5107-4588-9

Printed in China

CONTENTS

INTRODUCTION

I will be the first to admit that for the past twenty-five years, I've lived a double life. I even went as far as wearing a disguise and altering my appearance. Yes, it is true that during this time, I've played the role of Santa Claus for a local department store and most recently for a certain famous "Mouse."

There is one idea I always find fascinating when thinking about Santa—no matter how old we get, we still want to believe in his presence and the magic he seems to possess. For most of us, somewhere within the deep recesses of our mind, the concept of Santa Claus is remembered as a joyful and meaningful experience.

Santa Claus is the figure of hope that suggests there is still good and kindness in the world. He provides an escape for us to slip back into our childhood and forget all about the worries and burdens of being an adult. For those who have children, a visit to Santa Claus reminds us of the true meaning of the holidays.

I'm not saying that every visit to Santa Claus with the children, and even adults, has been picture-perfect for me over the years. That has been the fun part of playing Santa. Seeing my own three children hold me in high regard for my role as Santa has been one of my greatest experiences. Also, for my children not to realize it was me, as Santa Claus, has only added to the magic of their many visits.

Over the years, I have enjoyed the opportunity to share my story with others, beginning with how I secured the position of Santa Claus to some of the more memorable encounters with the Jolly Old Elf and some rather unique children.

How do I still recall these stories so well? Well, whenever I recounted a story to a friend or family member, they encouraged me to write it down. And so it was that I got into the habit of writing or organizing these stories in order to provide a system of recording and preserving their value. I guess you can say, this book has been a "work in progress" for more than twenty-five years.

The book examines the traditional Santa visit and helps answer some of the more basic questions that make up every child's visit to the man in the famous red suit. It tackles those traditional and burning questions such as *What can Santa get you for Christmas?*, *Are you leaving any milk and cookies for Santa?*, and, one of my personal favorites, *Have you been good?*

For years, I grappled with a title for this book. Originally I called the book simply, *True Confessions and Stories of a Department Store Santa.* However, the concept of being a department store Santa basically has become a dying breed over the years. Perhaps sadly, there are very few true department stores that feature a Santa Claus for children to visit anymore. The notion of Santa, or rather a visit to Santa, is generally considered now a visit to the local mall and meeting the Santa that is there on duty. When I was growing up in the 1960s and early '70s a visit to Santa Claus meant a trek or journey downtown. The concept of large malls was just in blueprint form when I was a youngster.

Growing up, I lived in Philadelphia and the downtown area was scattered with large department stores. You were either a Gimbels family or a Wanamaker's family, or even a Lit Brothers or Strawbridge & Clothier family years ago. I can remember Gimbels had an extensive toy department, while Lit Brothers featured a Christmas Village, and Wanamaker's topped them all with a real working monorail in the store and an elaborate light show.

These were the institutions and landmarks where most people from Philadelphia and the surrounding area would shop and it was also your home for the holidays when it came to a visit to Santa Claus.

My only memory of actually sitting on Santa's lap when I was younger, was me sitting and not saying a word. I was like Ralphie from *A Christmas Story* when he couldn't initially remember what he truly wanted for Christmas. (Of course, for those fans of the motion picture, we all know he wanted a Red Ryder carbine action 200-shot range model air rifle.)

According to my parents, apparently my older brother, Gerard, was the spokesperson for the two of us when we visited Santa Claus. So, I have no idea or memory as to what he asked for on my behalf. I do remember not getting my Planet of the Apes figures by Mego when I was seven years old. I was devastated. Every cool kid back then had them on their Wish List. I guess I wasn't cool enough.

Which brings me to another title that I toyed with for this book: *I Look Better Far Away*. This title has a meaning all to itself in its ability to describe the ideas or feelings of the children that patiently wait in line to see Santa. They are so excited and they can't wait to sit on Santa's lap and tell him about everything that is on their own wish list. However, as they move closer to the actual lap and the realization that they are about to see Santa close up, the element of fear and panic overtakes them. So, for many kids, myself and Ralphie included, Santa does really seem to look better far away!

But that's not necessarily true for every kid. And so it is that the final title seems to be most logical and the best description for the book you are about to read. I hope you enjoy the following pages as much as I did the journey in putting together and retelling these memorable stories.

WHY ME?

Many people over the years have asked me things like, *how did you ever get the job playing Santa Claus? Were you looking to be a Santa Claus? Was it a job you always wanted? Did you lose a bet?*

Then after I secured the position, the first question from most people was, *Did any kid ever tinkle, poop, pee, urinate, slabber, vomit . . . [the list or some version of the list or description goes on and on] on you?* Fortunately, in all of my years I can honestly say "no" to that line of questioning. Call it fast hands or just a pinch of luck. Maybe it's a little bit of both.

As for the question, "How did you get the job?" well, I guess you can say I was in the right place at the right time. In other words, I walked into the employment office and the hiring manager admitted to me that he had one final job to fill this holiday season, and then he could go on vacation. I was that guy, and I am sure the hiring manager had a wonderful time on vacation.

Interestingly, I was never told what the role was until the very end of the interview process. I learned from the hiring manager that there was this opening for the holiday season

and I would be perfect for the role. I, on the other hand, was in my second year of college and I was in search of a part-time job to help carry me through the Christmas season. I needed money because my father's wallet was running dry. I had thought about all of the places that I didn't want to work—for example, fast food establishments. I have nothing against them; it's just I figured I had flipped my share of burgers during my high school years.

So, where is a decent place for one to work for the holiday season? *How about a department store?* I wondered. *They should at least pay pretty well on an hourly basis, and besides, practically all of them offer some type of store discounts.* A store discount was a pretty big factor in my decision-making process because I knew I had a lot of Christmas presents to buy and every little bit helps. So, why not take the plunge? Fortunately, I was going in with an open mind, which meant I would take any job offered—sales, stocking the shelves—it really didn't matter to me.

Fortunately, the town where I lived, Philadelphia, had an abundance of big-city department stores. So, the next morning, I set my sights on visiting one such store's personnel department as soon as classes were completed for the day. The store's name was Strawbridge & Clothier, which sadly no longer exists. For decades, it was a Philadelphia institution, but as mergers and takeovers became the law of survival, Strawbridge & Clothier got bought out and it was slowly abandoned.

One plus about this particular downtown store was its location, and how easy it would be for me to get there from school. I was just a short bus ride away. As soon as classes ended for the day, I made my way to the store. As I got off the bus and crossed the street, I paused for a moment and looked up at the eleven-story building. The brightly decorated windows came into focus, depicting scenes of the upcoming Christmas season, which reassured me that I was at the right place.

I hurried to the nearest elevator and pressed the number eleven, the location of the personnel offices. As I approached the doorway, I took notice of all the other eligible candidates already filling out their applications. I could not help but wonder if they were my competition.

Trying to remain focused, I picked up an application at the entrance, where they were lying in a bin by the hundreds. I then carefully crammed myself into one of the many little wooden desks scattered throughout the room. I felt like I was back at Sister Dorothy's fourth grade classroom at Holy Child once again.

The application was nothing special. After completion, I presented it to a woman who was seated at a desk at the front of the room, who, from what I could tell, was there to evaluate and screen potential candidates. After glancing over my application for a grand total of five seconds, she put it down, folded her hands, and said, "Oh, we're all done hiring for the Christmas season for now."

What?! Did I miss that sign coming in the door? My face told the whole story. Then again, I knew she was probably programmed to make such a statement and must have said it a thousand times every day. As soon as my face began to regain some expression, I started to mutter under my breath. "Why didn't you tell me before I wasted my time filling out that crummy application?"

After inquiring to her again about the availability of work and was again told nothing was available, I turned and made my way to the door. I began to walk out and after only a few steps, I heard the woman's voice call over to me. Could persistence have paid off? "Wait a minute," she said. I turned and headed back to the desk and saw her ruffling through some papers. She must have found the one she wanted because after she pulled out this one in particular she asked me a rather unusual question, "Do you like kids?" That's a rather ambiguous question and why would she ask something like that?

After gaining my composure, I blurted out the only response that came to mind, "Sure, they're okay."

I guess that was all she needed to hear, because the next thing I knew she was asking me if I could come back on Wednesday, just two days from now.

"Sure, I don't see any problem with that," I said as I was still not entirely clear what was happening.

She then asked, "Is three o'clock alright?"

"No problem," I reassured her.

"Good, we'll see you again on Wednesday. Is it Kevin?" she said as she glanced at the application again to confirm.

Well, as you can probably imagine, from the moment I walked out of the office and for the next two days, a thousand different scenarios crossed my mind. To tell you the truth in my wildest dreams, I could never have imagined they were talking about a job as Santa Claus. I was nineteen, skinny, and had a kid face. Not to mention, it wasn't that long ago when I used to see the big man in the bright red suit myself. Becoming Santa was a long shot for me. What I did know was that Wednesday couldn't come fast enough and my curiosity was getting the best of me just waiting to find out what this whole thing was about.

It's funny, I was so curious I didn't even bother trying any other department store that day to see if they were hiring. All I knew was that I still had a lot of questions which needed to be answered and that they were the only ones who could give me those answers.

Wednesday finally arrived and I once again made my way downtown after my last class. Fortunately, even with a few minor travel delays, I made it to the store with a few minutes to spare. I approached the personnel offices and I once again observed the all too common scene—a room filled with job applicants filling out forms for future jobs. I guess they didn't get the memo yet that the store is done hiring for the holidays.

As I made my way up to the front of the room, I noticed the same woman who told me to come back was again seated at the desk glancing over applications. As I moved closer to the desk, the woman was the first to speak. "Oh, there you are Kevin, we've been waiting for you." *Well at least she remembered my name; that's a plus,* I thought.

"Kevin, I've scheduled you for a 3:15 appointment to see Mr. White, one of our hiring representatives. He will be with you shortly," said the woman as she glanced at a series of holiday season applications she was about to reject.

As I made my way toward the waiting area, I picked up a Christmas catalog, hoping to get myself in the Christmas spirit. Ironically, I turned to the toy section. All of the latest toys were scattered throughout the catalog along with some old reliable toys that have dominated catalogs over the years.

I began to reminisce about my own childhood and how I couldn't wait to get our copy of the Sears Christmas Wish Book. As a kid, the only pages that were of any significance were the back pages where you would find all of the wonderful toys. I could hear my parents saying to me, "Now, make sure you circle the toys you want so Santa knows what to bring you." I always did wonder why the toys came with prices next to them when it was Santa and the Elves who made them. Did Santa have a bank account, and if so where did he get his money from? Big questions for a little kid, but I was probably not alone. I thought back on my childhood days and how G.I. Joe was always the gold standard, not those 4-inch poseable action figures of today. I mean the twelve-inch guy with that same scar on the side of his face and that same fuzzy hair, beard, and moustache. I remember as the years went by, how G.I. Joe got a little more sophisticated as they added features, like the talking mode and even ones with Kung Fu grip.

Before I knew it, the time was 3:30 p.m. and there was still no sign of Mr. White. Just as I was putting down the Christmas catalog, the door swung open and out stepped a gentleman. He began to introduce himself to me while I remained seated, "Kevin, Mr. White here," as he extended his arm to shake my hand.

With a wide, sincere grin, he said, "Glad to meet you. Edna has told me all about you and has told me you would be perfect for the job."

Edna, Edna who? I thought to myself. I didn't question, but I would just listen for now. Keeping my inquiries to myself, I said, "Oh, thank you, Mr. White."

"Why don't you come in, Kevin? My office is right down the hall."

As I entered his office, I thought to myself, *Oh, not a bad office, he must be doing pretty well.*

"Come in Kevin, make yourself comfortable. Now, I do want to apologize for the delay. I just had a little unfinished business to settle first."

"No problem," I said, "just catching up on the Christmas catalog!"

I tried to remember my goal was just to listen for now and let him do all the talking, and that is exactly what he did.

Clearing his throat, Mr. White said, "Now, Kevin, Edna out front said that you're very interested in getting a job here with us for the holidays. I like that kind of persistence."

Well, I was right. All that nudging did pay off—or at least enabled me to get to Mr. White's office. My mind racing, a light bulb suddenly went off inside my head. The woman at the front desk was Edna.

With an eager nod, I answered him, "Yes, I am interested, but Edna said that nothing for the Christmas season was still available."

"Well, that is true and Edna does do her job well when it comes to letting the applicants know this. However, there is a position still available and it definitely has to be filled before Black Friday—the day after Thanksgiving."

This still did not curtail my growing curiosity.

Mr. White continued, "But, I will add, this is no easy position to fill, and it is not a position for everyone. So, in a way, Edna is correct when she mentions we are all done hiring for the Christmas season."

I didn't say a word, but I did add a nod here and there to show Mr. White I was still interested in this unknown position. Mr. White continued, "This isn't your run of the mill ordinary job."

As I sat and listened, my curiosity was getting the best of me. I thought I had to ask the question, "Who do I have to kill?" based on the level of excitement and specialty this position seemed to carry and one which I was apparently uniquely qualified to hold. I figured I'd let Mr. White finish.

"Kevin, as I mentioned, this job is not for everyone, it's actually the toughest for me, personally, to fill each year."

Again, I sat there listening, but, by this point, my attention began to wander. You know what I mean. You're at an interview and you have a million and one things that run through your mind. You're not paying attention at all. Then you think of a question, but at that point, you stop and think, *should I ask him, or did he just talk about that?* Finally, I caught up again with the conversation, thinking this guy is smooth, I bet he can sell ice to an Eskimo.

"Yes, Kevin, this job requires patience, good listening skills . . ."

What did he just say? There I go, wandering again.

"It requires a cheerful disposition at all times and the ability to think fast. And I'll be honest, it isn't easy having to deal with so many different types of people. An even temper along with stamina are also a must," Mr. White went on to sell this mystery job the best he could.

"However, there are certain advantages to this job compared with many other positions throughout the store. For example, good pay and we'll work around your schedule. I know you're in college so if you need some time off for midterms or exams, whatever it may be, whatever, let us know and we'll work around it. And lastly, Kevin, we'll have plenty of people around to help you out." Little did I know at this point he was referring to Santa's Helpers.

I was all ears, especially when he said the magic words that every college student wants to hear: good pay. Finally, my curiosity got the best of me, and I said, "Mr. White, you know I've sat here, and listened to you tell me about a job that sounds too good to be true. You know that I must be extremely curious because for one thing, when I originally filled out and handed in the application, I was told that nothing was available. Now, I go from one extreme to another with a job that only I can fill."

And, this time I said it jokingly, "What's the job and who do I have to kill?"

"Ok, are you ready for this one, Kevin?" Mr. White questioned as he prepared himself to reveal the information that I had been itching to know.

"Sure."

"It's . . . Santa Claus."

At first I thought he was joking. Then the worst thought crossed my mind. All I could imagine was that he was talking about me being an elf and having to wear a ridiculous pixie outfit, so I had to ask, just to clarify, "Do you mean an elf?"

Mr. White was a little surprised by my reaction. To clear up the confusion, he shook his head with a response, "No, I mean Santa Claus. You know, *Ho, Ho, Ho!* The old guy with the bright red suit. Jolly Old St. Nick, Kris Kringle with all the toys . . . the Big Guy who sits in the big chair while all the kids come up and sit on his lap."

"Santa Claus," I said, sitting there absolutely stunned.

My first reaction was that this is not the job for me. But, before I could reply with the statement, I stopped myself and fortunately said, "Well, why not? I'll give it a go."

This was not an answer I thought about too much; it just came out. Almost like it was supposed to happen . . . as if it was meant to happen.

With a wide grin, Mr. White said, "Great, I'll have Edna get all the necessary paperwork together for you."

Of course, with every big decision comes the doubts. My mind became clouded with thoughts about how I was not right for this position. I could not help myself from asking

Mr. White the two things that were bothering me the most. I needed to make sure this was not a mistake.

"But don't you think I'm a little young for the part?"

"Nothing that a little Santa makeup can't solve."

"But, what about my size? Don't you think I'm a little too skinny?"

With a nonchalant shrug, he replied, "That's why God made pillows."

There was nothing left to say. Trying to be confident that this was right, I said, "Well, Mr. White, you certainly make a good salesman. You've given every good reason that I should take this job. And, if you think I can do the job, that's good enough for me."

"No, thank you, Kevin. Believe me, I know I didn't make a mistake."

"Now, I guess you can relax, that Christmas vacation is pretty safe now."

So it was that, at nineteen years old, I became the youngest Santa Claus the store ever had. I may be a little older and slightly heavier these days, but I am still thankful for makeup and pillows. Over the course of those years, I've worked with many other individuals who have also played the role of Santa. Though they have all come and gone, I've stayed because it is a part of my own life story, and I'm not quite ready to close the chapter.

One page I had to turn came in 1996, when the department store, where I worked for the past thirteen years, faced their first corporate buyout. One of the many cutbacks that then followed was the elimination of their holiday Santa Claus. Sadly, this Santa was then without a home.

Fortunately, I reprised the role for twelve holiday seasons for a certain mouse and for a certain cruise line, where we live in Florida these days. I have concluded that Santa Claus is one of those love-hate kinds of relationships. It's not for everyone, but for me, it has been one thing: pure enjoyment. In the twenty-five years that I have played the role of Santa Claus, I have estimated I have seen in excess of 100,000 little kids and big kids alike, making up one tired Santa lap. I have heard the Christmas wishes from every age group—from newborns (with a little help from Mom and Dad) to a ninety-three-year-old great-grandmother.

My greatest joys have come from seeing the faces of my own three children, Matthew, Emma, and Grace over the years. They've seen me in the role, but the magic for me lives on because in all of their visits they never knew the Santa Claus they were visiting was their own good old dad. Now, they are a little bigger and only recently did they all stop believing in Santa. Rather, my children have reached the logical conclusion that Santa is a really nice guy and all that, but Mom and Dad have assumed the role over the years as primary gift givers.

I am basically retired these days from the role of Santa Claus, but I am hoping to put on the suit one day again when my children have children of their own and once again I can experience the magic and wonder of the holidays through their eyes. And, finally, to Mr. White, I never really did get the opportunity to say this back then, but, "Thank you, and I'm glad you gave me the chance."

"WHAT CAN SANTA GET YOU FOR CHRISTMAS?"

A t first glance, the question "What can Santa Claus get you for Christmas?" appears relatively harmless, but it's the all-important starting point of every Santa visit. After having experienced as many years of playing the role of Santa Claus as I have, what you learn is to expect the unexpected.

Over the course of many years, this Santa has heard his share of traditional requests as to what a child would like for Christmas from Barbie dolls to Teenage Mutant Ninja Turtles, computer games, Transformers, LEGO toys, action figures, American Girl dolls, and even board games (imagine that!). The list goes on and on.

This chapter, however, is dedicated to some of the more untraditional requests that have made their way to this Santa Claus through the years. The requests range from the practical to the absurd, but their responses reinforce the basic underlying belief that every child is uniquely different and is very much wonderful in their own right.

That is, in fact, one of the many reasons that I look back fondly on my twenty-five years of playing the role of Santa Claus. Many people have asked me why I continue to go back every year. The answer is simple—I love the job. I took an instant liking to the position. Since I was only nineteen when I started the role, one might argue that maybe there is just a little bit of Peter Pan in me, an individual that just doesn't want to grow up. On the other hand, who really wants to grow up anyway? I hear it's overrated.

Yet despite my admiration of the job, I quickly realized I needed a strategy when responding to kids. So it was that I put myself in the shoes of a five-year-old child all over again.

Sometimes, though, the plan required some adjustments as I learned things on the job. I remember an interesting phenomenon that occurred during the second year of playing Santa Claus. It was known as the Cabbage Patch doll. Parents all across the country were going crazy in an effort to find this doll. Shelves would empty as quickly as they were filled and demand certainly outweighed supply by titanic proportions.

This was when I learned a very important lesson when it came to playing Santa Claus—never promise a visiting child anything, unless you get the thumbs up or okay from a parent or guardian. I prepared myself for any child who asked for one that Christmas. Santa would say, "Santa's Elves are working extremely hard this year and therefore, Santa will do his very best."

You just can't make any promises. The reasons are simple. What if the child has had his or her heart set on getting this particular toy and you go ahead and promise. What happens on Christmas Day when that toy isn't there? Santa would be gone for another year and it's the parent's problem.

Yet those are the easier challenges. The big ones usually occur on the day traditionally known as "Black Friday" in the retail industry. In fact, I remember the very first day I played Santa Claus, which was, of course, the Friday after Thanksgiving—a day given the distinction of "Black Friday" because it is built on the hopes of all retailers that sales will be brisk enough on that single day to help put them into the "Black" on the books, representing a profitable year.

There I sat, waiting for my first child thinking confidently I was prepared so well to hear all about any toy any boy or girl

in *Kiddyland* could possibly ask for this Christmas. The time had come for this Santa to meet his very first visitor. Then the unexpected happened.

Little Karl, along with his mother and father, stepped right up for his visit. He was eager to tell Santa all about the wonderful things that he wanted for Christmas. Santa's Helper was the first to greet Karl and his parents. The helper asked the little boy what his name was and then proceeded to escort him to Santa Claus's chair.

The helper was the first to speak, "Santa, this is Karl and he would like to sit on Santa's lap and tell you about some of the things he wants for Christmas."

It's always good to use the child's name in the conversation as much as possible. In addition, having someone like Santa Claus's Helper get the child's name for you is a plus for any Santa. If the helper is able to get the name of the child for you, then it saves Santa from asking the child. Besides, it makes Santa look good because remember, Santa is supposed to know all, especially when it comes to names.

Then once the child is introduced to Santa, you can always turn the conversation around and make yourself look good by replying, "Of course this is Karl! You've certainly grown so much since Santa has seen you last."

[Note from Santa: There is another *Golden Rule* when it comes to playing the role of Santa Claus—you try to avoid the word "I." You speak in third person. One other thing I learned with regard to these greetings—though this one was more personal preference than a rule—was never to say *"Ho Ho Ho!"* I know the phrase has always been associated with the legend of Santa Claus, but I personally don't always seem to say it with quite enough gusto. I credit those Santas out there with the voice for it but for me, I guess I am more of a tenor. Yet I digress . . .]

After greeting Karl, it was now time for him to sit on Santa's lap and tell me about all the toys, games, and gadgets that he wanted for Christmas.

Karl's response to the question, which he communicated rather enthusiastically, was "Coal!" Startled by Karl's response, Santa's natural response back to Karl's unusual request was "Why do you want coal? Have you been bad?"

Knowing the legend behind Santa and coal, I figured it was a legitimate question and felt this was perhaps a confession on Karl's behalf.

Somewhat startled by Santa's question, Karl replied, "No, Santa."

Santa was determined to get to the bottom of this one and asked again, "Then why do you want coal for Christmas, Karl? Coal is generally given to little boys and girls that have been bad."

Confident with his answer, Karl blurted out, "Because Santa, I want to bury the coal and in ten thousand years I'll have a diamond!"

Clever, very clever, I thought, but not at all practical when you think about it. Well, Karl certainly provided this Santa with a rude awakening, an awakening that taught me an early and valuable lesson that out of the mouths of babes does come the most unexpected. So from that point on, I remembered what Karl said to me, and welcomed those untraditional requests.

Yet every child is different, and for many children, simplicity can also be a necessary and wonderful ingredient. Take, for example, Julia.

"Potatoes, I want potatoes," replied Julia to Santa's traditional request regarding Christmas gifts.

Naturally, I thought to myself, *Julia must be a little confused*. So seeking to clarify Julia's response I asked, "Oh, you must mean a Mr. Potato Head!"

"No, just potatoes."

I guess Santa Claus should have asked, "Do you prefer Russet, or Red or Yellow potatoes, or even Santa's favorite Fingerling potatoes?"

Yet another clever request came from Benedict, a little boy just about six years old who knew all too well that his "wish list" (the traditional name for a list of toys a child wants for Christmas) could be classified as excessive.

However, this was not going to deter Benedict and his list. To Benedict, there was no real reason to prioritize. He wanted toy number fifty-nine just as much as toy thirty-two or seventeen. So as Benedict finished up with his wish list, he turned to Santa and said, "Oh don't worry Santa about my list, my daddy has a big truck if you need any help."

Oliver and Cody also came for a visit to Santa Claus one day with an extensive wish list. Oliver spoke on behalf of the two of them when he said, "Hey Santa, here's our list. We don't expect you to bring everything; it's twelve pages long!"

In these cases, Santa Claus had to remain very excited at the notion of such a wonderful list. Santa then turned to the boys and asked, "What is the one toy that is most special to you for this Christmas and that you want Santa to bring you?"

Otherwise, Santa would be there for an hour reading this list.

A little girl named Anastasia was much more diplomatic when it came to her wish list and what she wanted Santa

Claus to bring her for Christmas. She said, "Santa, I would love this doll, but it is much too expensive for you to bring all of her accessories. I will be happy with just the doll."

I remember saying and thinking to myself, *How sweet!* These are the children that realize the true meaning of the holidays and are happy with whatever you bring them for Christmas.

A little boy named Luke came to visit Santa Claus one day and asked for the following, "Santa, I want a chimney for Christmas."

Santa naturally replied, "Do you want a chimney for Christmas so this way Santa can use it when he visits your house on Christmas Eve?"

Then I got this look back from Luke as though Santa had just asked the mathematical equation for the theory of relativity. "No," replied Luke. "I need a chimney to hang my Christmas stocking!"

Then there was Gabby, who also had her heart set on just one thing. This is how Gabby's story goes:

Gabby approached Santa's chair accompanied by Santa's Helper. She was a charming little girl of about seven. Very polite, a lot of "yes, Santa" as I continued to ask her questions. Then came Gabby's opportunity to let the big guy in the bright red suit in on the one item that was on her wish list.

"What can Santa get you for Christmas this year Gabby?" asked Santa.

"I want a hot tub, Santa."

The first thought that crossed my mind was, *Why?* and *Where did she hear this?* Was it some effective advertising campaign she saw or was this just a clever way to slip in a request for Mommy or Daddy? Either way, you just kind of sit there and shake your head.

Then there was Darnell. In 1983, Eddie Murphy produced a comedy television show for HBO called *Delirious*. In it, he spoke about kids having a fascination for the smell of Brut cologne, and I believe this was the case with Darnell.

"What can Santa get for Darnell this Christmas?"

"Brut."

"What?"

"Brut."

Santa, being an Eddie Murphy fan himself, replied kiddingly, "Brut by Faberge?"

"Yeah, that's it!"

"Darnell, would you like Santa to bring you anything else for Christmas?"

"Nah, that'll do it."

Another thing I learned during these discussions is that children can be easily influenced. Whoever said that they aren't hadn't met Karen and Joey. Let's start with Karen, a five-year-old who came to visit Santa one particular Christmas season. Karen couldn't stop talking about her idol, Elvis Presley, that day. *What a cool kid*, Santa thought, from one Elvis fan to another. Naturally, Karen's request was centered on the King of Rock and Roll. Specifically, she asked for the "entire Elvis Presley CD collection." Whoever said the King is dead?

Joey, on the other hand, had a different pop culture idol: heavyweight boxing champion Mike Tyson. But why Mike Tyson?

"I like his gold front tooth!" said Joey as he then proceeded to ask Santa for a gold tooth just like his hero's for Christmas.

But the kids' knowledge of the world extended far beyond pop culture, I'd soon learn. Take Sharon, for instance. Santa asked little Sharon exactly what he could bring her for Christmas and her response even surprised Santa.

It turns out that Sharon really didn't want much, just "a Visa and a Mastercard." She also asked if the two could come with "no limit."

Not to be outdone by Sharon's request, Isabella asked Santa for "a briefcase full of money."

What a change from the days when I was a kid! When I was younger, it seemed like our only concern was getting together enough kids to play a game of baseball or football. As for what toys always seemed to dominate my own wish list, Lincoln Logs and LEGOs ranked pretty high.

I was always fascinated with the toys that could build things. I never asked for clothes (in fact, I hated clothes with a passion, but what kid really likes them?). You certainly don't want to be in a situation where you waste a wish on clothes. I wanted to reserve those few precious spots on the list for toys.

Then, once in a while, there were those kids who would come along and melt my heart with their requests. Robert was one such example.

"Santa," Robert said, "I know you're busy and all that stuff, but maybe someday can you come out and watch me play baseball?"

I wish I could have said yes to Robert, but you have to follow the *Golden Rule* and you don't want to make any promises. Although, I do love baseball! Robert did, however, bring up a very valid point in his follow-up line of questioning: What does Santa do in the off-season, especially during the summer months? I know Santa is responsible for his "Good Book" and "Bad Book" (I never used the word "naughty" when I talked to the kids, so "Naughty List" and "Nice List" were not part of the vernacular) and supervises the toymaking process, but be realistic, even Santa requires a vacation now and then.

Sometimes, it became clear to me that there were more society-wide problems exposed by the answers to Santa's question. Violence and weapons seem to have always had a place on children's wish lists, though the traditional game of cops and robbers to which we were exposed while growing up has undergone some changes over the years. Now it's warriors, ninjas, warlords, attack forces, and even contras. What hasn't changed is Mom's opinion on the subject. I think Eric brings this point across rather nicely.

According to Eric, "Santa, there is something else I would like for Christmas. I would like a Rambo doll, but my mommy doesn't want any guns in the house."

I did get a request from a little boy named Bruce, who asked for a BB gun. Of course, the first thing I thought of when Bruce made the request was the movie *A Christmas Story*. After looking up at Bruce's mom, I could tell immediately he wasn't about to get his request in a million years. I wanted so much to say, "You'll shoot your eye out!" but I thought that was better left for Mom and Dad to say.

Something else that hasn't really changed much over the years is that no matter the age or race of a little girl, dolls are always the most requested item from Santa Claus each year. The one that tops the list every year is, without a doubt, Barbie. Truly, I've got to hand it to Barbie. Even after all these years, she is still able to enchant and thrill each and every little girl. You've got to admit, Barbie has held up pretty well. Not one wrinkle after all this time.

It is within the Barbie category that I've often gotten the most unusual requests.. Take for example, Ella, who was having a little problem with her Barbie.

"What can Santa get Ella for Christmas?"

"Some Barbie clothes," replied Ella.

Logically Santa asked, "So does this mean you have a Barbie doll now, Ella?"

"Yeah, but she doesn't have any clothes."

Sadly, all I could imagine was this naked Barbie running around.

Then there was Lacey, who happened to be in desperate need of a new Barbie doll when she came to visit Santa one Christmas. The tears in her eyes gave it away.

"Lacey, why are you crying?" asked a concerned Santa Claus.

Hysterically Lacey replied, "My Barbie doll."

"What about your Barbie doll? What's the matter with her?" again Santa was curious to get to the bottom of this dilemma.

Lacey then pointed her finger at her twin sister and said, "Lori ripped her head off!"

Apparently, Lori was seeking revenge from an earlier incident and decided to use Lacey's Barbie doll as the instrument of her rage.

Jasmine had a similar problem with her Barbie and was hoping Santa could help.

Santa questioned, "What else can Santa get Jasmine for Christmas this year?"

Jasmine replied simply, "Some Barbie pieces."

Somewhat confused by Jasmine's request, Santa pushed on and said, "Oh, do you mean some Barbie accessories, like a Barbie car or dream house?"

Looking at Santa this time like he was crazy, Jasmine replied, "No, I need a new leg and an arm for Barbie."

Finally to conclude my tribute to Barbie, there was Zoe, who seemed a little confused concerning the subject of anatomy. Zoe couldn't have been any older than four when she paid a visit to Santa Claus one Saturday afternoon in December.

Speaking in a gentle voice, doing my best not to startle Zoe, Santa asked, "Can Santa get Zoe anything special for Christmas?"

"I want a girl Barbie and a boy Barbie," replied Zoe.

Over the years, this Santa has also heard his share of unusual wishes, but they fall into the category of simple requests. I know that promising a child that you will bring a certain item for them for Christmas is a definite "no-no" but in Chadwick's case I thought I could handle the request.

"What can Santa Claus get Chadwick for Christmas?"

Chadwick replied, "Air."

Santa's only reply back given the request was, "I think I can handle that!"

Then there was Russ and his request from Santa, which went something like this:

"What special thing can Santa bring Russ for Christmas?"

"A box."

I guess it's true when they say the kid will probably like the box more so than the toy that came in it.

There was also Daryl, who asked Santa for the following after being questioned. "I want macaroni and cheese!"

Again, I think I could have handled that one.

I'm pretty sure I could have handled Agnes's request as well.

In response to Santa's question, "What can Santa get you for Christmas?" Agnes said, "I want rope for Christmas."

Naturally, Santa thought Agnes was referring to jump rope, so I questioned her response.

"No, just rope," Agnes replied.

Similarly, there was Logan, who just asked for "string."

There was also Eddie, who was probably thinking more about breakfast than his Christmas list when he asked for "an egg and cheese sandwich."

Another classic request came from Victoria when she asked for "blue toys." Victoria never did go into any detail as to which blue toys she meant, but apparently this four-year-old's favorite color was blue and she didn't care which toys Santa Claus was going to bring her as long as they fell into this color category.

And finally, there was Dylan, who after Santa's question, "What can Santa get you for Christmas?" replied, "A haircut."

I felt like saying, "Hey, does this kid know I'm not a barber or hairstylist!" This is when Dylan's mother stepped into the picture and told Santa that her little boy wanted to look like Mr. T. For all of those folks out there who are not familiar with this individual, here's a little history:

Mr. T was one of the stars of the 1980s television program *The A Team* who could easily be distinguished by his trademark Mohawk haircut. Well, luckily for Dylan, this was one request I was certainly not going to promise, considering the look on his mother's face at the slightest hint of a haircut such as that.

However, not all of the requests were so simple. Then, there was the other extreme.

For instance, Phil asked for "all the toys in the local shopping mall." There was also Felicity, who requested "a briefcase full of money." Tyler asked for his house to burn down. When Santa Claus asked the logical question, "Why?" Tyler responded, "This way I can ask you for a fire truck so I can put the fire out." And finally there was Luna, who phrased her response to Santa Claus's question, "What can Santa get you for Christmas?" as simply, "I want everything."

Another unique request came from Elizabeth, whose wish I was not about to fulfill.

"Elizabeth, is there anything else you would like Santa to bring you for Christmas?"

"Yes Santa. A new baby sister."

"Oh, you mean a little baby doll, don't you?" Well, at least Santa Claus is consistent. I was wrong again!

"No, I mean a real baby sister."

"Elizabeth, you're going to have to ask your mommy and daddy for that one." Another excellent example of why Santa doesn't promise anything.

A popular request year after year seems to be for appliances. I don't mean appliances like the Easy Bake Oven, a toy kitchen, vacuum cleaner, lawn mower, or even a snow cone machine, I mean those manufactured by Whirlpool, Hoover, LG, Sony, BLACK+DECKER, and Amana. And speaking of vacuum cleaners, kids always seem to be fascinated with them. Maybe it's the noise vacuums make or the way they clean up messes. I'm not really sure, but until some company out there makes one that is silent then kids will continue to request them from Santa.

What I have discovered is that, in most of the cases, the reason appliances are part of the Christmas wish list is because they want to help Mommy or Daddy with some chores around the house.

A perfect example of a child wanting to help one of their parents with chores was Owen. While speaking to Owen one Saturday morning a few seasons back, Santa asked, "Now Owen, what can Santa get you for Christmas?"

"A saber saw; Daddy has some paneling to do around the house and I want to help him."

Louie asked for a collection of tools but then followed it up with this interesting promise back to Santa.

Louie said, "Hey Santa, if you leave me all of the tools I want, I promise to clean your clothes every day!"

I honestly didn't have a reply to Louie at this point.

Then there was Rose who said, "I want a vacuum cleaner."

Santa's response back was "One that is made so when you

walk with the vacuum cleaner, the top lights up?" I really thought I was being clever; I had just seen one like it and thought maybe Rose meant the same one.

"No," replied Rose, "a real one from Dyson."

This desire to help out Mommy, Daddy, and other family members also extended to the dinner table. For example, there was Jessica, who decided the Thanksgiving turkey could use a little sprucing up.

Here is how the story went, according to Jessica's mother, when she told Santa the tale on Black Friday many seasons ago. It was Thanksgiving Day and Jessica had asked if she could help her mommy and grandmother prepare the special meal. Well, at some point, both mom and the grandmother left the room to greet some other family members who had just arrived. Jessica, who was just about five, decided the family's turkey looked a little dirty. Jessica did the next best thing and took the turkey over to the sink and decided to give it a bath, utilizing water, some dish soap, and a sponge. By the time the mother and grandmother both got back to the kitchen they noticed the turkey was completely immersed in soap and bubbles, and even a little cleaner.

While Jessica's turkey story may have been more unusual, there were some requests that I heard on more than one occasion. As mentioned earlier, dolls, especially those named Barbie, have always been popular with little girls over the years. The best plain old doll request I can recall came from Cassidy, who simply requested, "Santa, I want a doll with a lot of hair."

No doll in particular, just one that had a whole heap of hair.

It was 1985, and I was in my third year of playing Santa Claus when a new plush doll made its entrance in the marketplace. The new doll was known as Teddy Ruxpin. What made this doll so popular with kids was that the bear's mouth and eyes moved while it read stories that were played on an audio tape which had a cassette built directly into its back. It was a pretty cool toy for its day based on the technology that it utilized.

What Santa discovered was that, based on the number of requests I received that year and into the next Christmas season, the talking teddy bear was basically universal, and equal numbers of boys and girls wanted Teddy Ruxpin for their Christmas list. As you might have expected, Teddy Ruxpin is now the star of the next few stories.

To give you a little more history on Teddy, he was this brown two-foot bear that wore a tan vest. Again, you'd place a cassette tape in a compartment in his back and this would activate the bear's mouth and eyes which would allow him to talk. Teddy would talk and talk and talk.

Derek offered a perfect example of how important it was to give Teddy Ruxpin a rest every once in a while.

"I want a new Teddy Ruxpin doll," Derek asked when prompted.

"A new one? What happened to your old Teddy Ruxpin?"

"My daddy ripped the old one's mouth off."

Tammy had a similar problem, but it involved her mother and Teddy Ruxpin. Again, Tammy phrased her request in the same fashion as Derek, and she too wished for a "new" Teddy Ruxpin. Tammy responded, "I want another Teddy Ruxpin doll because my mommy broke it. She said she was tired of hearing it!"

In Grayson's case, his parents decided to attack Teddy Ruxpin's life-support system. Grayson was hoping Santa could help him out with this problem.

"I want batteries Santa, because my mommy and daddy hid the ones that go into my Teddy Ruxpin doll."

Some kids sure are clever! In another such example that illustrates why Santa Claus never makes any promises, a little girl named Morgan must have practiced her response over and over again, "Santa, I'm going to give you one more chance this year. This time last year, I sat here and asked for some ballerina slippers and you didn't get 'em for me! This year I want them again."

I didn't have the pleasure of seeing Morgan for a third year.

Maybe, it was two strikes and you're out for Morgan. She just wasn't about to give this Santa another chance.

Now, I haven't yet addressed the topic of live animals. The answer is yes, kids do request them, but don't think of the traditional domestic animals if you ever plan to play Santa; think exotic and global.

Little Heather, for example, requested from Santa, "two hermit crabs." And Tracey wanted a goanna! I had to look that one up when I got home. I did find out it was a lizard primarily found in Australia. There was also Don who asked for a "boa," and if I couldn't get one of those then a "lizard will do." For little Bubba, a dog and a cat were not enough.

"Go ahead Bubba, tell 'em what you want for Christmas."

"A real elephant."

[Note from Santa: Bubba is just one of many nicknames I came across during my time as Santa. Other nicknames included Boogie, Eggy, Egghead, Skeeter, Limpy, Tubby, Pooh, Rocky, Roo, and my personal favorite, Boo-Boo.]

But back for a moment to the subject of pets, I can't forget about Garrett. From what I could surmise, the family's pet cat had just died so in Fluffy's remembrance, Garrett requested the following from Santa.

"Santa, can you help me get my cat Fluffy stuffed for Christmas?"

Apparently, the parents had just gone through a divorce and Garrett thought this would be an easier way for them both to enjoy Fluffy. Garrett also thought this was the perfect way to transport Fluffy from house to house.

Kathryn was another child who asked Santa for a new pet; this one was a feather friend for Christmas, namely a parakeet. Somewhat concerned and assuming the worst, Santa asked, "What happened to your old parakeet?"

"He got out of his cage and Daddy accidentally sat on him!"

Oh no, I thought . . . splat, poor Polly.

Don't get me wrong, on occasion you do get your share of requests for dogs and cats for Christmas. Little Pam provided Santa with just such a request. This is how the conversation between Santa and Pam went.

"Well hello, Pam. You have certainly grown since Santa has seen you last. Was there something special you would like Santa to bring you for Christmas?"

With a big smile on her face, Pam replied, "A kitty cat."

Santa then asked, "Would you like a real kitty cat or a stuffed animal kitty cat?"

"It doesn't matter, they're all the same!"

I'll end on one final cat story. Paul asked Santa for a cat. That wasn't unusual in and of itself, except for the fact that the family already had one and when they moved, I guess in the hectic pace they forgot kitty.

Over the years, some of the more touching requests you get from children involve items they want Santa to bring for their parents, sisters, brothers, and other family members. Many of these children feel as though these other family members might be left out of the whole Santa process. So as not to disappoint, the child generally does the requesting and wishing for them.

The requests usually come at the tail end of their own wish lists. The children generally tell you about the wonderful things they would like and once they get their requests out of the way, and locked in, they feel free to do the ordering for the rest of their family.

"Mary is there anything else you'd like Santa to bring you for Christmas?"

"No Santa, but I would like you to bring a case of Schaefer for my daddy."

Brian, on the other hand, was looking out for both his parents when he made the following request, "Santa, if it's no trouble can you please get my daddy a Jeep Cherokee and my mommy a winter coat?"

Wow! It seems like good old dad is getting the better of these two gifts. But since Santa's role is not to offer commentary, I'd learned to keep my opinions to myself.

Vonnie was actually looking out for the rest of the family when she decided that air freshener was an appropriate gift for her little baby brother. As Vonnie put it, "I think you ought to get Russell an air freshener for Christmas, Santa, because he doesn't smell that good."

Lincoln, on the other hand, was looking out for an older sister when he asked, "Santa, can you help my sister get her driver's license and help get the band U2 to play at her birthday party?"

Then there was Anna, who was looking out for her aunt when she asked Santa for "two carrots for my Aunt Danica."

I don't think Anna meant "two carrots" that one might find at your typical farmers market, but rather at Jewelers' Row.

On several occasions each year you do get a big brother or big sister looking out for the younger ones. So it came as no surprise to this Santa when Christopher, age five, sat up on Santa's lap and began to ask for something for his little sister.

"Santa, I think my sister Colleen would like a new rattle."

"That's very thoughtful of you Christopher to be looking out for your baby sister. Doesn't Colleen have a rattle?"

"Well she did, but daddy's van ran over it."

Frank also thought that he was looking out for his little sister when he asked for a "muzzle for his sister." I think the crying by his sister was getting the best of Frank.

Children will also often request presents for their beloved pets. The best request that this Santa has heard over the years was from Brooklyn, who had a little dog that she loved dearly. So naturally a request directed to Santa Claus for her doggy was certainly appropriate. Brooklyn phrased her request something like this, "I want a tree for my doggy."

Walt was a little boy no older than six, who decided it was time for Santa Claus to get a gift for his pet hamster.

"Walt, is there anything you would like for Christmas?" questioned Santa.

"I would like a new metal spinning wheel for my hamster."

How nice, but why a metal wheel? Santa wondered. I guess I'd better ask.

"But why a metal wheel?"

"Because Sparkle keeps biting through the plastic one."

Adam asked Santa for another little puppy because he thought the family's other dog needed company. Adam, however, was reluctant to actually request a new dog because, in his words, "I want another dog Santa, to keep Spooner company, but Daddy said that he'd leave the next pet I bring home on the highway."

Santa instinctively thought Miley was making a request for her dog as well when she said, "Santa, I would like a pooper scooper for Jack!"

Naturally, Santa asked the next question, "Is Jack your little doggy?"

Wrong again, Santa! "No, Jack is my little brother."

Then there was little Joe, who requested, "Can you stop Chewy from pooping on the carpet?"

Before we leave this subject and the age-old question, "What can Santa get you for Christmas?" I don't want to forget the last category of individuals who have come and visited Santa Claus, and in most cases sat on my lap.

The group I am referring to are the "big kids"—those adults out there who have faithfully taken the time to visit old Saint Nick. The notion or idea of Santa must pull some emotional cord in these big kids during the holiday season and they begin to think back to their younger days and attempt to recapture the feeling of Christmases gone by.

So, not to disappoint this collection of bigger kids, Santa Claus plays along. They generally get a picture and then let Santa in on some of their requests. What's so funny is that the smaller kids in line don't think anything is suspicious or wrong with an adult sitting on Santa's lap. They figure adults want toys too and Santa is the same guy who fills their requests.

I must say of the adults who do come to visit Santa Claus each year, I really do enjoy their visit. As you might expect, some of their requests are quite memorable as well.

Take for example Al, an employee at the department store this Santa has been working at for years. Al has been one of this Santa's more faithful visitors year in and year out. Al was eighty-two the first time he came to visit Santa. Every year, Al makes one request.

"Now Santa, I've been pretty good, so how about getting me a blonde for Christmas?"

Unfortunately, each year Santa has to disappoint Al when he replies, "Al, wouldn't that be a little messy trying to get down the chimney?"

I must say, Al takes it pretty well. I know I'd be disappointed too, but Al seems to have a good time with the request every year.

Generally, the ladies that visit Santa each year have expensive taste. How can you blame them? If you're going to wish, you might as well wish big.

Take Lorraine, who was following the traditional routine of wishing big. Lorraine popped by one evening prior to closing to visit Santa and said, "Hey Santa, how are they treatin' you today?"

"Oh, pretty good. How about you? Are you all shopped out for today?" asked Santa after noticing that both of Lorraine's hands were clutching shopping bags full of Christmas presents.

By this point Lorraine was sitting back and relaxing on Santa's lap.

"Yeah and my feet are killing me," said Lorraine.

"Well Lorraine while you're here, would you like Santa Claus to bring you anything for Christmas?"

"Why not. Do you think you can get those Elves working on a brand-new black Ferrari? Heck, I'll even take a used one."

Emily also came to visit Santa at the conclusion of a busy day of shopping and like Lorraine had some rather expensive tastes.

"Emily, how can Santa help you today?"

"You know, big guy, there is something you could get me for Christmas even though I haven't been good. How about a red-hot Porsche 911?"

Sandy thought Santa could play the dual role of match-maker and gift-giver when she paid a visit one Christmas season. Playing along, Santa asked the question, "What does Sandy want for Christmas this year?"

Sandy responded, "I don't want too much Santa, just a new man in my life. I kicked the last one to the curb a couple weeks back."

Leigh figured Santa and his crew of Elves were probably going to be too busy to make anything special for her, so she decided to request the basics.

"Hey Santa Claus, how about a stack of fifties for Christmas?"

Obviously, this Santa has heard a similar request a time or two before as my response to Leigh's question will indicate, "As soon as Santa gets back to the North Pole I'll have the Elves print them up!"

[Note from Santa: Marvin had first phrased his request to Santa this way, "Remember Santa, I want all of the gold in Fort Knox." So it was that I learned from the best how to most appropriately respond to such requests.]

Zoey, however, was concerned about Santa's well-being when she decided to ask for an air-conditioned suit for Santa. She figured this would be the ideal gift Santa could deliver to himself.

Santa thanked Zoey for her generosity and concern. And, I know, I mentioned before that I love the job of playing Santa Claus, but to be honest, the wool suit, beard, hat, boots, and the hot lights and flash from Santa's camera does sometimes create a rather pressure cooker for me at times. So, an air-conditioned suit would be an ideal addition to my wardrobe.

On most occasions, grown-ups get the biggest kick out of seeing Santa Claus and you can see it in their faces. To satisfy the grown-up desire to be a kid again Santa often turns to the parent or adult and asks them the similar question, "What can Santa get you for Christmas?"

It is my basic belief that grown-ups actually have more fun at times than the children, and their requests have certainly reflected this trend. Oftentimes, when a family is there to get a picture with Santa, I will ask the children what they would like for Christmas and then I usually turn to the parents.

Asking the parent about their own wish list serves two purposes—it allows the parent or adult to experience the Christmas tradition of seeing Santa again and secondly, by asking this simple question this reconfirms to the child that Santa is for real. However, I believe Evelyn's mother took Santa's question too seriously. After Evelyn told Santa all about the wonderful toys she wanted for Christmas I then turned to her mother and father to ask the question, "What can Santa get you for Christmas?"

Naturally, I was expecting the usual reply, such as "peace, happiness, and a healthy family." Well, it was at this point in the conversation that Evelyn's mother decided to let Santa in on what she really wanted the big guy to bring her. "There is something special I would like for Christmas, Santa. There's this black bra I saw in the window of Victoria's Secret that I would just kill for!"

You can understand why I was left speechless. I felt like saying, "I don't remember if black bras were available this year. I know red bras were popular with the Elves this year but not black."

I've also noticed that adults love to admit to Santa that they have been bad, especially the women. They seem to think it is an appropriate time to confess to anything when they are around Santa Claus. I know Santa is derived from Saint Nicholas, but ladies I'm not a priest. For example, Allison's reply to Santa's question went something like this: "If I told you Santa what I really wanted for Christmas, then I'd be on your naughty list!"

Olivia's reply to the traditional Santa question had many similar qualities.

"Santa, I can't tell you that! I'm not sure whether it is legal or not."

Then there is a group of individuals out there I truly feel sorry for each Christmas season. They are the guys who come with their girlfriends to what they think is just an innocent visit to see Santa Claus. The guy thinks that a visit to see Santa with his girlfriend is going to be a great way for the two of them to capture that Christmas spirit.

What he doesn't realize is the guilt he will eventually receive once his gal pal reaches Santa's lap and how the visit was actually all part of some grand scheme.

Allow me to set the table for you, as played out at least four or five times each Santa season. The couple visits Santa Claus for that ideal Christmas picture. The girl will generally sit on Santa's lap and the guy will kneel on the floor beside the two of us. The picture is taken and not to disappoint any on-lookers as well as to keep the tradition alive Santa will ask the question, "What can Santa get you for Christmas?"

Like clockwork, the girl is always the first to speak. She turns to Santa and then to her boyfriend, points and replies, "For him to give me an engagement ring!"

So there she is, still pointing at her boyfriend and of course he's speechless, the most he can muster up is a shrug of the shoulders, mouth open and then the sluggish reply, "oh, man."

So guys, heed my warning. If you are not ready to pop the question, be very careful when your girlfriend innocently asks you, "Wouldn't it be fun to see Santa this Christmas?"

But sometimes, magic is in the air for couples visiting Santa. Take Kevin and Sue, a couple both in their mid-twenties who decided that this particular Saturday in December, a few seasons back, was the perfect time to see Santa Claus. For the two of them, the visit and picture with Santa was going to be the ideal backdrop to their Christmas. Kevin was the first to speak, letting Santa know that this marked the fourth visit over the years by the two to see this Santa.

Touched by their loyalty Santa replied, "Welcome back, I'm glad that you've made Santa one of your Christmas traditions."

I guess I should have figured something was a little different when Kevin replied in a peculiar fashion. "You can call it that if you'd like."

By this time, Sue was sitting on Santa's lap while Kevin had positioned himself next to the two of us on the floor. The picture was taken, capturing the special moment, and then I decided to ask the standard question as to what the two would like for Christmas.

Kevin, still kneeling on his one knee, turned to Santa and then to Sue and said, "For her to marry me, Santa."

Santa truly thought he had heard it all until then. At first, I wasn't sure if Kevin was serious, but then I quickly knew his request was certainly no mistake. The most I could come up with was, "So, what will it be, Sue?"

Sue, by this time, had already put her hands to her face and was crying.

Kevin then mentioned how much he truly loved her, and how he wanted her to be his wife and that he would be the happiest man on earth if she would spend the rest of her life with him. You know, all that mushy stuff.

Sue was still crying, hands still to her face, however she did begin to nod and blurted out a somewhat inaudible, "yes, yes, yes . . . "

It was at this point, some of the crowd waiting patiently to see Santa, figured out what was going on with the couple. In the background you could hear the "Ahs" echoing from the crowd. You might be asking yourself, what was I doing while this was going on? The answer, absolutely nothing. I became somewhat of a spectator, but with front-row seats.

Then all of a sudden Kevin reached into his coat pocket and he pulled out this engagement ring. By this time, word had reached everyone in line and then I noticed Santa's crew of helpers just watching with smiles as well. When Kevin pulled the ring from the coat pocket the crowd seemed to respond in harmony with one loud and collective "Ah." Kevin placed the ring on Sue's finger and repeated his desire for her to be his wife and with that the crowd, the helpers, and Santa all broke into applause.

It did occur to me later that night when I was retelling the story to my family and friends, I may have been one of the few men in the history of recorded time to have another guy propose to his girlfriend while she was sitting on my lap.

Unfortunately, I never did receive an invitation to Kevin and Sue's wedding. Though to be fair to the couple, mail to the North Pole can be rather slow at times!

DEAR SANTA . . .
LETTERS AND ARTWORK FOR SANTA

Over the years, this Santa has received thousands of letters from children detailing their Christmas wishes. For many children, the letter is an important part of their visit to Santa. Each child takes extensive time and care to craft and detail those toys they most want for Christmas. It also helps the child gather their thoughts better, especially when most children are very nervous at this special meeting with Santa. The longest letter this Santa has ever received featured 112 toys covering 17 pages!

When they are given the opportunity to share their letter with Santa, the child experiences a level of great joy. To add to this level of excitement, Santa will often say to the child, "Santa is so glad you brought him your letter. Can Santa take this letter back to the North Pole with him to show Mrs. Claus, the reindeer, and all the Elves?"

This is very important stuff to most children that Santa will be spending this much time with their letter.

I do remember a little boy named Juan, who, when asked the question "Can Santa take this letter back to the North Pole with him?" said, "No, Santa! I'd rather you didn't. I've grown kind of sentimental to the letter."

Drawings presented to Santa Claus have also been very popular over the years. But, children's art is as unique and individualized as each child is different. Santa often has to ask them what they have drawn and sometimes I take a guess at the picture as to what it could be. Most of the time I am wrong.

Take for instance Gracie, who gifted Santa a beautiful picture she drew.

Santa said to Gracie, "Wow! This is a beautiful picture."

"Thank you, Santa," she replied with a proud grin on her face.

"Is this a picture of you, Gracie?"

"No," replied Gracie. Strike one.

"Is it Mrs. Claus?" I already knew by this point it was strike two and I continued to be wrong.

"Is it Santa Claus?"

"No," said Gracie once again and it was strike three at my end.

"Then, who is the picture of Gracie?"

Gracie then replied, "It's Kim Kardashian, Santa. Can't you tell?"

"Oh, that was Santa's next guess. The next time Santa is

out in Beverly Hills he will stop by and visit the Kardashians and show Kim and Kanye your beautiful picture. Would that be okay?"

"Thank you, Santa."

Another one of Santa's favorites features no name, just a list of items the child would like Santa to bring them for Christmas. Interestingly, the child started out with good intentions, asking for sunglasses, clothes, jewelry, and even a remote control car but then decided they would just keep it simple for Santa Claus by asking for "Cash"!

The next letter emphasizes one of the greatest fears of any child who comes to visit Santa Claus. They are well aware of Santa's "all-knowing" ability when it comes to his "Good Book" and "Bad Book," but they are suspicious of his use of GPS.

In this case, David wanted it to be clear that he would like any delivery of toys on Christmas Day to arrive at Nan and Pop's house.

Then there's the question of a child's definition of being "good," which doesn't always parallel to those around them. According to Kathleen, she believed she had been well-behaved, but acknowledged that regard for such behavior might depend on who you talk to.

I truly enjoy the next letter, because Gilbert captured the true concept and understanding of what the holidays mean. However, when he began to play the role of a "judge" and attempted to tell Santa Claus all about his sister's behavior, this is when he got into some trouble.

According to Gilbert's mother, his sister wasn't too pleased by her younger brother's letter, and in her words, how he was "snitching to Santa Claus" about her in his postscript. She then did the next best thing and scratched out the comment by Gilbert of how she "has been bad."

The next letter is short and sweet, but very effective. If I were to guess, the letter was probably written while waiting in line to see Santa Claus. If I were a betting man, which I am not, I would imagine the child, in this case named Sandra, realized she had no list for Santa Claus. The ambitious parent with them then grabbed the first piece of paper available to them and jotted down the requests of their child. Problem solved!

The first side says it all; they "tried to be good" and it was very polite to include Mrs. Claus on the letter. It also ends on a cliffhanger, meaning you have to turn the page over to see the contents of the "wish list" and the toys Sandra would like Santa Claus to bring her for Christmas.

I love the next letter because it helps to showcase how some of the sweetest children that this Santa has seen over the years request things for a parent, guardian, grandparent, or loved one and not for themselves.

In this case, Gabriel knew presents for his mommy ("dress," "matching shoes," and "pocketbook") were more important than any present Santa Claus could bring for him.

The final piece of artwork comes from Matthew, who has a true appreciation for the *Star Wars* universe and how he believes a lightsaber battle between Santa Claus and Darth Vader would be the ultimate battle of good versus evil.

Interestingly, Santa Claus, in the artwork, is seen carrying a red lightsaber. Does that mean he is susceptible to the dark side? Santa Claus is also a huge *Star Wars* fan.

"DON'T FORGET THE MILK
AND COOKIES!"

"Are you leaving milk and cookies for Santa when he visits your house on Christmas Eve?" is the perfect close to every Santa Claus visit. What I mean by the word "close" is simply my way of bringing the negotiation between child and Santa to an end. It's a necessary evil, so to speak, for any Santa. Normally, you'll have a multitude of children waiting to see Santa on any given day and as much as you want to spend as much time with each of them, every visit must come to an end.

There have been many stories as to the origin of "leaving milk and cookies" for Santa. Some point to the medieval German tradition of the paradise tree. Other suggest the custom began during the Great Depression when it was believed that even children must be able to experience the concept of sacrifice. A more exotic meaning points to Norse mythology and the god Odin and his eight-legged horse Sleipnir. While others believe the tradition began with Saint Nicholas himself when it was customary to leave a treat in exchange for a gift.

Well, whatever the reason, it remains the perfect ending to every visit to Santa Claus. I'll be the first to admit, in our house, we still leave milk and cookies on a special plate we put out every year on Christmas Eve for Santa Claus and even though our three children are teenagers now we've done this routine every year.

So, after the children sit on Santa's lap and tell him all about the wonderful toys they would like for Christmas, Santa then asks them if they are going to leave Santa Claus the traditional serving of milk and cookies when he visits their house on Christmas Eve.

Legend has quite a bit to do with this question as well. Knowing that Santa has to travel to all of those houses and cover such a great distance, milk and cookies provide that much-needed energy for Santa Claus to continue his journey.

Sometimes, when we'd get to the "milk and cookies" part of the conversation, Santa would get some funny feedback.

In one example, Kelly was a girl no older than five, well-behaved and mannered and one that would certainly never tell Santa Claus a fib. I'll pick up the conversation after having determined what Kelly wanted for Christmas. It went something like this:

"Santa is so glad you stopped by to see him today. Remember Kelly, if you can think of anything else you would like Santa Claus to bring you for Christmas, you can always write him a letter at the North Pole."

Politely Kelly replied, "Thank you, Santa."

"Remember Kelly, don't forget to leave Santa some milk and cookies when he visits your house on Christmas Eve, will you?"

"Sure, Santa," Kelly responded sweetly. "But, I'm going to leave the milk and cookies in the refrigerator 'cause we have roaches."

You can certainly imagine poor Kelly's mother who just heard those tender innocent words from her daughter. Needless to say, embarrassment is an understatement. Maintaining a straight face without a hint of laughter was an accomplishment for this Santa.

Kelly provided another perfect example of just how kids say the darndest things.

One of my personal favorites, however, involved Mason. Mason's visit to Santa was another example of a mother's worst nightmare, or, one more example of how a mother could go from the joy of seeing her child with Santa, to embarrassment. Again, I'll start at the conclusion of Mason's wish list.

"Well, Mason, Santa will do his best to bring you what you want for Christmas but remember you have to continue to be good!"

"Yes, Santa," replied Mason.

Santa then went in for the close, "Mason, are you going to leave Santa some milk and cookies when he visits this year?"

In an emotional response Mason said, "I'll leave the milk, but not the cookies, and, do you know why?"

Picture if you can, Mason was sitting on Santa's lap and aggressively pointing his index finger at me while asking the question, "And, do you know why?"

Before ever being given the opportunity to respond, Mason added his reason for not leaving the cookies. "Because cookies are not at all nutritious and they are full of sugar!"

Naturally, the first thing that crossed my mind was, I wonder how many times this same statement had been said to Mason! It was at that point I decided to look up to Mason's mother and ask.

"Just curious, how many times has this been said to Mason?"

Mason's mother really didn't have to say a word, the answer was written all over her face, but she did add, "Oh, about a hundred million times."

Then there was Liam, who thought Santa may prefer a little something different as opposed to the traditional feast of milk and cookies.

Again, I will pick up at the end of my visit with Liam after having determined what his Christmas wish list was, "Well Liam, that certainly is a big wish list for Santa. Santa will do his best. As always, it was nice of you to stop by and see Santa today. Are you going to leave some milk and cookies for Santa when he visits your house on Christmas Eve?"

Liam pondered the question for a moment and then the answer came to him. "Hey Santa, how about some Chex cereal instead of the milk and cookies?"

In a supportive tone, Santa responded, "Sure, they're okay."

I could detect the expression of relief on Liam's face before he voiced his true intentions, "Good, because we're trying to get rid of them. Grandma keeps bringing them over and nobody likes them!"

In terms of other untraditional treats which Santa has been promised over the years, the story of a child named Noah comes to mind. Noah must have thought it can get a little hot in that big red suit that Santa Claus wears and thought he could use a cold one.

"Now remember Noah, if you think of anything else you would like Santa to bring to you for Christmas, please by all means you can write Santa Claus a letter at the North Pole."

"Sounds good," Noah replied confidently.

"Noah, are you planning to leave Santa some milk and cookies when he visits your house on Christmas Eve?"

With Santa's best interest in mind, Noah simply asked, "How about a Colt 45, Santa?"

"Wow, malt liquor!"

From Santa's perspective, he is strictly a hot cocoa kind of guy.

Several years back there was Abby, who thought Santa could use a good hot meal during his long travels.

"Remember Abby, if you can think of anything else you would like for Christmas, you can always write Santa a letter at the North Pole. And, once Santa receives your letter, he shows it to Mrs. Claus, then to all the reindeer and especially then to all the Elves so they'll know what to make for Abby for Christmas."

[Note from Santa: Yeah, I know what you're thinking, pretty corny. But remember, when Santa gives that much attention to your letter and you're only four year old, that's a big deal.]

"Abby, are you going to leave some milk and cookies for Santa?"

"Sure. Santa, if that's what you want, but how about some nice macaroni and cheese to go?" replied Abby.

Not bad! You can't beat macaroni and cheese, no matter your age.

I will always remember Ed, who asked Santa, "What's your favorite type of donut, Santa?"

That is my kind of kid, as I can always go for a good donut!

Then there was Mia, who for some reason got Santa confused with her puppy.

"It was so nice to see you today, Mia. Santa was so glad you were able to take the time out of your day to come down and see him. Now Mia, are you going to leave Santa some milk and cookies when he stops by your house on Christmas Eve?"

"I'm going to leave you milk, cookies, and a doggy bone."

From what I can remember, Mia never really gave any clear indication as to why a doggy bone was part of Santa's late-night snack routine. I'm sure they'll be good for Santa's teeth and hopefully it will keep up my shiny coat.

Over the years, I have also been promised such liquid treats as Coca-Cola, Mountain Dew, Pepsi, Dr. Pepper, coffee (to help keep Santa awake for his busy night), Gatorade (to restore those lost vitamins and minerals), a milkshake from McDonald's, and just plain water. Interestingly, no one in all of my years has ever offered to leave me a cup of hot cocoa.

As far as those culinary treats, they have ranged from a Philadelphia hoagie, to French fries, fruit roll-ups, tacos, pizza, fudge, an egg roll, a soft pretzel, gummy bears, fajitas, a sundae, chicken tenders, spaghetti and meatballs, and even fondue.

Then there was a little boy named Hector, who stopped by to see Santa one Saturday in December a few years back. Hector was especially concerned at the physical condition and well-being of Santa. Hector was, needless to say, a weight-conscious six-year-old.

"It was certainly nice to see you today Hector, and remember if you can think of anything else for Christmas, you can always write Santa or even come back and visit him again."

"Thank you, Santa."

"Now Hector, are you going to leave some milk and cookies for Santa when he visits your house on Christmas Eve?"

With some concern in his voice Hector responded, "I don't think so, Santa."

Curious, Santa asked, "Why?"

Hector then explained his reasoning, "You know Santa, it's important for a man of your age to watch your weight. So I'm not going to leave you any cookies, but maybe some fruit and some skim milk. What I mean Santa is, you're fat!"

Aiden was one child who didn't want to take any chances and he wasn't about to make any promises of his own involving the milk and cookies until he got some type of guarantee from Santa Claus.

Playing the role of encourager, Santa said, "Now Aiden, you have to continue to be good and always do what your mommy and daddy tell you to do."

"All right, Santa!" Aiden replied with some hint of sarcasm.

"Do you think you are going to leave some milk and cookies for Santa when he visits your house on Christmas Eve?"

Aiden replied, "I'll leave the milk and cookies as long as you leave the presents."

Clearly, we had a future negotiator in the making.

And, let's not forget Chloe, who also wasn't about to make any promises either as long as her big brother Christian was around.

"Chloe, I can see that you've been a good girl and Santa will certainly do his best to get you what you want for Christmas."

Chloe responded softly, "Thank you, Santa."

"Chloe, do you think you will be leaving some milk and cookies for Santa?"

"Sure, Santa, I'll leave the milk and cookies, but if they're not there when you get to my house don't blame me, it wasn't my fault. Blame my brother, Christian, he's promised to eat them."

Then there was Sophia, who was happy to leave Santa some milk and cookies but thought that some mashed potatoes would also go well with Santa's late-night snack.

One of the more unusual treats that Santa has been offered over the years came from Diana. It must have been my first or second season as Santa Claus when Diana came to visit.

When I finished asking Diana about all of the wonderful toys she wanted for Christmas, I posed the question about Santa's milk and cookies.

Diana responded by asking Santa if he would prefer some fresh cantaloupe instead.

Brittany asked Santa if he liked Chicken à la King, Vinny preferred to leave pasta e fagioli, and Lila asked if Santa would have time to eat a piece of Boston cream pie when he came to drop off her toys on Christmas Eve. Then there was Sabrina, who wanted to leave a Thai wax apple for Santa. Though I think that might be a better gift for Santa's reindeer.

That brings us to little Jacob, who was determined not to leave Santa with any milk or cookies during his visit.

Being the inquisitive type of individual that I can be, I asked, "Why not?"

"Because last year when I left them, Tikki ate them all and got sick and threw up the whole next day!"

After some additional questions, Santa found out that Tikki is the family's German Shepherd dog, and milk and cookies were not part of her diet.

Along the same lines of the traditional request for milk and cookies, Santa often asks children who visit him if they plan on leaving any treats for the reindeer. Yes, let's not forget those reindeer! They get hungry too, and they work just as hard.

[Note from Santa: However, don't ask me to name those reindeer. That's right, I'm embarrassed to admit it, but I've played a Santa Claus for over twenty-five seasons and I still don't know all of the reindeer names. I know there's that little jingle and of course, the classic Gene Autry song that plays in my head every season, but I just have the toughest time remembering. One day perhaps, I'll know them all. I just get a little confused after Donner, Blitzen, Comet, and so on . . . !]

One Friday night four or five seasons ago, when Rachel came to visit, she too expressed some concern about the reindeer and decided that a little roughage was a necessary part of every good reindeer's diet. In addition, Rachel thought that Santa could use some too. I figured at least it would help keep me regular.

"Remember, Rachel, if you can think of anything else that you would like to tell Santa, you know you can always write him a letter at the North Pole or even come back and visit Santa again."

"That sounds fine, Santa," Rachel responded excitedly.

"Rachel, are you going to leave some milk and cookies for Santa when he comes to visit your house and maybe even a carrot or two for Santa's reindeer?"

"I'll leave the milk, but how about some spinach for you and the reindeer? It's not fair that I have to be the only one who has to eat that stuff!"

Charlotte, on the other hand, expressed concern about Santa and his reindeer.

"Santa will do his best to bring you what you want, but remember, you have to do your part and continue being good for your mommy and daddy."

"All right, Santa, I will," said Charlotte.

"Are you going to leave some milk and cookies for Santa and possibly a carrot for his reindeer when he comes to visit you on Christmas Eve?"

"Santa, I'm going to leave milk and Oreo cookies for you and some pickles for your reindeer," replied little Charlotte.

I could only imagine what was going through Marian's mind when she came to visit Santa one particular day.

"Marian, are you going to leave some milk and cookies for Santa when he comes to visit your house on Christmas Eve and maybe something for my reindeer?"

In a sweet little voice Marian replied, "Sure, Santa, I can do that, but what about some mint chocolate chip ice cream for your reindeer?"

Well, I've already told you about Chloe, who wasn't about to make any promises concerning the likelihood of leaving milk and cookies as long as her big brother, Christian, was around. Then there was Aiden, who was only going to leave the milk and cookies if Santa left the "loot" under the tree. Then there was Jeremy, who too wasn't about to make any promises.

"Now Jeremy, Santa can tell that you are trying to be a good boy. Therefore, Santa will do his best to get you what you want for Christmas."

"It's a deal," responded the great negotiator.

"Santa is so glad that you were able to stop down here today and visit with him. Are you going to leave some milk and cookies for him when he visits your house on Christmas Eve, and what about a carrot or two for Santa's reindeer?"

Jeremy's response to all of this was simply, "We ain't got no carrots and I don't think we're about to get them anytime

Illustration Credit: Grace Neary

soon. And as far as the milk and cookies, I'll leave them under the chimney, but if you step on them, it's your own fault."

This section wouldn't be complete if we didn't recount what Carter had to say when Santa asked him that all too innocent question, "Are you going to leave some milk and cookies?"

Carter's reply to Santa's question was an unmistakable and unambiguous, "I hate milk, so the answer is no!"

EVERYTHING YOU WANTED TO KNOW ABOUT SANTA BUT WERE AFRAID TO ASK

Curiosity is the cornerstone of every child. The need and desire to ask questions about the world around them is embedded in their very nature. Their various levels of curiosity have extended over the years to questions pertaining to every aspect of Santa Claus. Questions have been about my red suit, my white beard, my age, where I live, my large jolly old belly, and my marital status.

One question that seems to arise every few years or so pertains to my reindeer. It goes something like this, "Why doesn't Santa ever introduce new reindeer to his crew?" The question always seems to make its way to Santa after the annual broadcast of the traditional holiday program, *Rudolph the Red-Nosed Reindeer*. I guess it is fair to say we've all seen the movie. The 1964 stop-motion program has become a holiday classic after first appearing as a book published in 1939 for the Montgomery Ward department stores.

In the show, they talk about this Reindeer Training School. It is at this school that we are first introduced to Rudolph along with a collection of young bucks and new recruits hoping to impress Santa Claus enough to make it to "The Show." Ironically, this is also the place where the other reindeer didn't want Rudolph to partake in the festivities. The question remains, why have this Reindeer Training School if you aren't going to introduce any new members into Santa's crew? It's the same original eight each and every year. Those eight seem to have a lock on all eight positions and are highly unlikely to give them up.

Yes, I know what you're thinking, and it's true that Rudolph was eventually added to the team. Remember, the only reason he was placed at the front of the team was because of his bright red nose. What many people don't realize is that Rudolph was introduced to us as Donner's son on the program. Given that Donner is one of the original eight, it would seem the whole Rudolph incident is a clear case of favoritism.

Then there is the case of the other reindeer. Initially, as mentioned, they don't want Rudolph to partake in the reindeer activities. However, as soon as Santa Claus shows some interest in Rudolph they conveniently invite him into their inner circle. They are just a bunch of toadies to Santa Claus if you ask me, but I digress.

One of the most frequently asked questions came from Wendy. Several years back this little girl, no older than four, visited Santa and asked the question which had troubled many before her.

Wendy asked, "How does Santa find the time in one evening to visit all of the houses and deliver all those toys to all of the children in the world?"

A very good question and one that many of you out there have probably been wondering yourself. My answer over the years goes something like this:

"Santa has the ability to freeze time. Santa freezes time and as time stands still, he visits all of the children in the world." I think that's a sound answer.

Early on, I'd really get into it and I would say, Santa starts out on the other side of the world and because they are a day ahead of us, he then works his way back to this continent and then in theory he has two days to deliver all of the toys around the world.

However, by this time you usually get a child that is sitting on your lap with this "what are you talking about" look across

his or her face. So, I know I will forever use the Santa freezes time theory as my out.

Another question you can always count on at least a half a dozen times each year concerns my beard. The question usually sounds something like, "Hey Santa, why do you have that big beard?"

My traditional response has been, "I have this beard because it gets so cold up at the North Pole and the beard keeps Santa warm."

Did you ever wonder how Santa is able to fit down all of those chimneys, especially when a house doesn't have a chimney? Well, this very same question was troubling Andrew.

"Santa, how are you going to fit down our chimney? We ain't got one! And besides, our roof is slanted to the one side."

Think fast Santa; I had only a minute to come up with an acceptable and believable answer. "Well, Andrew, in these situations Santa makes arrangements in advance with your parents. They wait up for Santa Claus. This way they can open the door to your house for him. This is how he is able to deliver all of those toys for the children out there who don't have chimneys. Do you understand?"

"Oh, I get it."

With that, I too breathed a sigh of relief. Naturally, this question has come up on more than one occasion and in each case, I answer the child in pretty much the same manner. I do, however, remember the time it backfired on me, with young Scarlett.

Apparently, I had told one of Scarlett's friends, "Santa Claus will meet your mother and father, and this way they can open the door of your house for Santa," who in turn relayed the explanation to Scarlett. As her parents explained it to me, Scarlett was absolutely terrified at the notion of Santa Clause coming to her house and her parents meeting this strange man at the door. I was told Scarlett wanted no part of Santa Claus, especially the thought of him in her house.

To keep peace and not to spark any future trauma in little Scarlett, Santa replied, "So, Scarlett, if it helps, I assure you I will drop off your presents down the street. This way your parents can go down and pick them up a little later." I also assured Scarlett that Santa Claus and his sled, along with his reindeer, wouldn't even fly anywhere in the same airspace as her house.

Now Chris, on the other hand, was the polar opposite of Scarlett. He loved the idea of Santa bringing all those toys to his house. So grateful was Chris, a little boy no older than five when he came to visit Santa a few seasons ago, that he also presented Santa with a gracious and lovely invitation with one stipulation.

After telling Santa Claus about all of the wonderful toys he wanted for Christmas, Chris said, "Santa, you know you're welcome to come over to our house for dinner anytime you'd like!"

Feeling a little choked up by this invitation, Santa politely replied, "Well Chris, that is certainly very nice of you."

Being somewhat proud of himself, Chris simply said, "I know." Then came the warning by Chris, "But, if you do come over for dinner, make sure you keep those reindeer out of our refrigerator."

Then there was Luca, who thought he'd make Santa's job a little easier. Luca was quite aware of the fact that his house did have a chimney but based on Santa's size there was a pretty good chance he wasn't about to fit down such a small opening. So he thought he'd break the news gently to Santa Claus one day when he came to visit.

The conversation began with my usual request, "Now Luca, you've come all this way, is there something you would like Santa to bring you for Christmas?"

"Yes, Santa, but I hope you're not going to get upset with what I am about to say, but I don't think you're going to fit down our chimney because you're too fat! But don't worry Santa, we've got a big backyard so you can park the sled out there and leave the toys there!"

Speaking of my sled, I have also been asked my share of questions concerning this magical flying machine and device. Take Avery, for example, who was particularly concerned about Santa's sled and its hauling capacity.

"Santa, have you ever looked into getting a bigger sled?"

"No, I really haven't, the one I have now is the original sled and it has worked well all of these years. And when you have a good thing going, you stick with it."

Kyle wanted to know what was the top speed Santa's sled can actually travel.

Ruby was curious if this was always my sled or did I get some upgrades to it over the years. I guess she wanted to make sure Santa had the latest model so there would be no danger of breaking down while I was attempting to deliver her presents.

Veronica wanted to know if Santa would ever consider painting the sled a different color.

There was also Cole, who expressed some concern about the payload and hauling capabilities of Santa Claus's sled.

Cole knew there was a whole lot of kids out there in the world who wanted something special for Christmas, but he wasn't sure how everything was going to fit into the sled.

So, Cole decided to ask the question, "Santa can all of the toys fit in your sled or do you have to make several trips back and forth to the North Pole to load up?"

As far as my answer to this question, I don't remember the exact words I used, but what I did say reassured Cole that the sled was larger than he thought and the Elves do an amazing job of packing.

Similarly, Adrian wanted to know if the sled ever got too heavy for the reindeer to fly.

Obviously, Eric must have watched his share of *Star Wars* movies and asked Santa Claus if my sled could reach lightspeed.

Maria was concerned about Santa's safety and naturally asked the following question, "Santa, does your sled have safety belts?"

Sebastian, on the other hand, was curious as to the whereabouts of Santa's big red toy bag. Sebastian asked, "Where is your red bag full of toys, Santa?" I can only imagine that the true authenticity of any Santa Claus is judged in many children's minds by his big bag of toys.

So, after Sebastian's inquiry I requested that a bag or some reasonable facsimile be placed at Santa Claus's display and therefore made a permanent fixture. Soon, a bag was added by the store to provide that level of comfort and reassurance to those worrying little ones who might have expressed the same concerns as Sebastian.

Playing the role of Santa Claus as long as I have does allow you to have your share of loyal visitors that come and visit you as the Jolly Old Elf each and every year. One such regular visitor over the years was a sweet little girl named Melanie. Amazingly, in Melanie's case, she had been a loyal visitor of this Santa for her entire life. Melanie is one of those children who came downtown with her parents to make the special trip to see this Santa each and every year. Remarkably, Melanie was actually in her teens when she stopped visiting Santa Claus.

I will always remember Melanie because of the great collection of questions she always had for Santa Claus each year.

One such question from Melanie went something like this, "Do all of the toys start out black and white and then Santa adds the color?"

Now, there's a clever question. Melanie somehow related the magic that's behind Santa with his ability to bring color into the world. In this little one's mind all of the toys start out dull and boring, then along comes Santa Claus, who adds the magic of color.

Another question thrown Santa's way by Melanie concerned all of the toy stores. "Does Santa make all of the toys that you find in the toy stores and online?"

I guess Melanie was wondering whether these toys were sanctioned or approved by Santa Claus or were they just 'Black Market' products! Or perhaps, Melanie asked the question to determine if this action by the toy stores was forcing some of Santa's Elves out of a job. Well, whatever the reason, I hope that Melanie will always maintain her high degree of curiosity and imagination.

The final and most recent question to come from Melanie concerned Santa Claus and his reindeer and their preferred choice of Christmas Eve treats. Melanie wanted to make sure she was leaving the right snack at her house for Santa Claus on the big day. Now Melanie knew that Santa enjoyed his milk and cookies but wanted to double check with Santa as to what type of cookies he preferred and what tasty selection would be appropriate for his reindeer.

Melanie asked, "What type of cookies do you like best, Santa? And what do reindeer eat? What should I leave for them?"

"As for which flavor and what type of cookie, Santa prefers oatmeal with raisin and his reindeer prefer carrots and apples but sometimes a little granola." I thought I'd add granola to the list; it sounded pretty convincing, and Melanie thought so too.

Speaking of reindeer, I have also been asked my share of questions concerning them. For example, Lindsay was curious about the ages of Santa's reindeer and expressed her question this way: "Aren't those reindeer getting too old to fly Santa? And by the way, how do they fly anyway?"

In defense of Santa's reindeer, I replied, "Don't worry, Lindsay, they are younger than you think and besides they practically know the route by heart after all these years anyway."

Interestingly, the next little girl in line heard my answer and decided to ask a question about the reindeer all on her own.

Brianne didn't quite understand this whole Rudolph the Red-Nosed Reindeer phenomenon. Brianne's conversation with Santa went something like this: "I heard what you said to that girl, Santa."

Thinking the same question had been troubling Brianne, Santa replied, "You did. Have you also been wondering about that question?"

"No, but what's with this Rudolph and the nose that lights up? And, is Rudolph real?"

Santa Claus phrased his response something like this, "Brianne, Rudolph is as real as all the rest and his bright nose often helps Santa Claus guide his sled."

Isaac was a little boy about seven years old who very much believed in Santa's reindeer and their ability to fly, but still had a question: "Do some of your reindeer fly better than some of the others?"

Addison wanted to know if any particular reindeer was considered the leader of the team. Not to play favorites, Santa assured Addison that no one reindeer is more important than any other and each year they take turns being the leader.

Another question which I get all the time is "Where are your reindeer now?"

In an effort not to disappoint the children, I explain to them that the reindeer are here today, but they are on the roof sleeping. Naturally, they immediately look towards the ceiling and say, "They are? Can I see them?"

Then, I have to break it to them very carefully that the reindeer have to get their much-needed rest because they have a long trip back to the North Pole later today. I must admit that the children, as a rule, do understand and are sympathetic to the needs of the reindeer.

However, the day came when I used this line one too many times. Apparently, I told Jason the same story when he came to visit me the previous year, when I said they were on the roof sleeping.

Jason reminded me that I may have used that excuse one too many times when he replied, "That is what you said last year, Santa. All they do is sleep!"

When I played Santa Claus for the cruise ship, I would have to phrase my response a little differently. Marinette asked the same question as to the whereabouts of my reindeer, and Santa replied, "They are certainly here today, but they are on the top deck of the ship near the pool sleeping."

Santa Claus discovered quickly he needed his sled with him, even more so when I worked on the cruise ship. How else could Santa have been there on Christmas Day, especially on a moving ship?

Interestingly, in the twelve years I did work for the cruise line, the day Santa worked and met with children and families was on Christmas Day and not prior. Knowing that, I was often placed in a situation where I had to explain to the children Santa will be contacted by your mommy and daddy when you get home. They will then make arrangements with Santa Claus and his Elves to deliver your presents. This was necessary because most parents were not in a situation where they would bring their children's entire bag of toys with them while they were on the cruise. So, when Christmas morning arrived, little Johnny and Susie's toys were not always there. A Santa's job I guess is never done.

Every once in a while, you get a parent who wants Santa Claus to do their dirty work for them. Take for example, the little girl named Megan and her mother who came to visit Santa a few seasons back. From what I could tell from my conversation with Megan, she had asked her parents for a dog, but they were definitely against the idea. When Megan asked for a reason why she couldn't have a dog, her mother replied, "Santa doesn't carry live animals on his sled."

Megan, however, was a little smarter and too persistent to settle for this excuse so she decided to ask the same question to Santa Claus when she came for her visit.

Megan turned my way and with this inquisitive look on her face asked, "Santa, is it true your sled doesn't carry live animals? I want a doggy!"

Figuring I needed to walk carefully through this answer, I looked toward Megan's mother for some kind of signal. The mother was standing directly behind Megan and was shaking her head "no." One could easily read her lips, "no dogs." I was stuck! How could I turn this around so I wasn't the bad guy?

My response to Megan went something like this: "Traditionally, Santa Claus does carry live animals, but this year at the North Pole the weather has been extremely cold and harsh. So Mrs. Claus and I have decided for the safety of all the dogs and other animals, we will not be able to deliver them to the good little boys and girls this year. Do you understand that we are doing this for their own protection, Megan? This way we can keep them safe."

Megan nodded yes back to Santa Claus and I felt as though I did my part to please both child and parent.

Speaking of letting Santa do the dirty work, some parents use Santa Claus as a way of correcting behavior. It's all part of the "Good Book" and "Bad Book" concept children seem to know. I do, however, enjoy helping a child with his or her passage from babyhood to their next stage of development.

Allow me to explain. This situation occurs at least three or four times each Christmas season. A parent or guardian approaches Santa's chair with their little one. The little one then removes the binky or pacifier that is in their mouth and hands it to Santa Claus.

Little Anthony was a perfect example of one such child. He and his parents came to visit Santa Claus and apparently Anthony was reluctant to give up his most treasured possession, his binky. From what I surmise, Anthony's parents thought his attachment to his binky had gone on a little too long and Santa would be the perfect accomplice to helping with the removal of the mouthpiece.

His parents turned to Anthony, as he stood just a few feet from Santa, and said to their little one, "Anthony, isn't there something you would like to ask Santa?"

Anthony replied, "Santa, can you take my binky back to the North Pole so you can give it to another baby who might need it?"

Santa said back, "That is very sweet of you Anthony. I will be happy to do so and I promise I will find your binky a new home."

Anthony then handed the saliva-filled binky over to Santa, saying not a word. He sadly walked away as though he had lost an old friend.

Every once in a while a question surfaces about the North Pole. All children seem to know about the North Pole and what a wondrous place it must be. Every child knows that it is Santa's home, that it is where Mrs. Claus also calls home, and it is where the magical Elves make all of the toys.

One of the questions about this mysterious oasis came from Chance, who inquired, "Is it really cold up in the North Pole?"

Nino asked, "Do you live at the North Pole all year long?"

"Can I ever go back with you to the North Pole?" asked Brent.

Then there is that all too familiar question, "What does your North Pole look like?"

Susie asked an excellent question that I must admit floored me when I heard it and I still don't know how I managed to wiggle my way out of it. Susie questioned, "How can you live up at the North Pole when there is no land mass?"

Phil, on the other hand, must have had some aspiration of being a letter carrier when he asked Santa, "How long does it take for a letter to get to you at the North Pole?"

As for the mysterious place known as the North Pole, the best question came from Hannah. Hannah went through the traditional Santa visit, she introduced herself to Santa's Helpers, she sat on Santa's lap, instructed him as to what he could bring her for Christmas, and agreed to leave milk and cookies. But just before her visit to Santa Claus was over she asked, "What does your house at the North Pole look like and how long does it take you to get home every night?"

Santa's reply first had to describe what a beautiful place Santa and Mrs. Claus live in and second, stress what a distance it actually is to the North Pole. If I didn't phrase the response correctly, then Hannah would have wanted to go with Santa and see for herself. Therefore, Santa replied, "Hannah, the North Pole is a very beautiful and wonderful place for Santa, Mrs. Claus, the Elves, and the reindeer. It is, however, quite far and extremely cold. But don't worry, over the years we've all gotten used to it there. As for your question, how long does it take me to get home, remember that Santa is able to freeze time and travel time is nothing at all."

Many children have questions about Santa's Elves. I guess they want to make sure Santa Claus is treating them correctly.

For example, the best question I remember about Santa's Elves came from Amelia. Amelia was concerned about the well-being of the Elves and wanted to be sure that Santa was providing a decent standard of living. So Amelia asked the question, "How much do you pay your Elves?"

Another clever question about Santa's Elves came from Christy. Knowing that Christmas would soon be here, Christy asked, "What does Santa get the Elves for Christmas?"

Yes, the Elves, those unsung heroes of Santa Claus. They do all the work, they design, create, and build all those wonderful toys, and the big guy, the toy god, Santa Claus, gets all the credit. Another one of those unsung heroes is Santa's wife, Mrs. Claus. Not much is known about Mrs. Claus. Perhaps the only thing is that Mrs. Claus is faithful, kind, and very understanding, and because of her obscurity many children seem very interested in knowing more.

A little girl named Rebecca came to visit Santa Claus one December afternoon and wanted to know a little bit about my faithful wife. Rebecca's question to Santa went like this: "When is Mrs. Claus's birthday? Because I would like to send her a card."

Another creative question came from Austin, who wanted to know what Mrs. Claus's name was prior to marrying Santa Claus.

Along the lines of Austin's question came an interesting question from Maritza. Maritza was a little girl no older than four who asked Santa one year, "How long have you and Mrs. Claus been married?"

Playing the role of the now forgettable husband, all I remember saying was "Santa and Mrs. Claus love each other so much we never count the years."

Some of the other questions, concerns, and comments about Mrs. Claus that have been asked over the years include "If you ever get sick Santa, does Mrs. Claus deliver the gifts?" Shannon wanted to know, "Does Mrs. Claus ever leave the

North Pole?" and Greg asked "Do you and Mrs. Claus have any children?"

Over the years, the children have also asked their share of personal questions concerning Santa Claus. For example, Stella wanted to know, "How long did it take to grow that beard?"

Anne Marie asked the familiar question, "How old are you, Santa?" Naturally, my response has been, "Santa Claus is ageless."

Summer, being the up and coming "influencer" that she was, asked a few years back, "Santa, can I find you on Facebook or Twitter?"

Quite possibly the thing that fascinates a child the most about Santa is his ability to know when they've been "good" and when they've been "bad." They are true believers when it becomes part of the legend that Santa possesses this ability to know their secrets and therefore keeps a record to track each little child's progress.

Tom, a little boy of five, came to visit Santa a few seasons back and was very curious about his own standing in Santa's "book." Tom said, "I know that you know when we've been bad or good. I've been trying real hard this year to be good . . . so I'm just wondering which book I am in."

I remember a troubled little girl named Clarissa who came to visit Santa Claus a few seasons back. Obviously, Clarissa had been bad or had been up to some mischief because the first thing that she said to me when she arrived on Santa's lap was, "Is it true Santa that you are really watching us?" Apparently, Clarissa had just been told this prior to her visit by her parents about Santa's "all-knowing" ability.

Perhaps the strangest question that has been asked to this Santa came from Dwayne. He simply wanted to know, "What if Santa dies?" How devastating! Then I asked myself if Dwayne knew something I didn't know or was planning something here?

Little Dave came to see Santa just a few seasons ago and had a question in reference to Santa's ability to know what each boy and girl are doing. Dave knows that Santa has a "Good Book" and a "Bad Book," but his question involved this "all-knowing" and "all-seeing" ability that Santa has. Dave wanted to know if Santa had a Magic Mirror that allowed him to see exactly which boys and girls have been bad or good.

Then there was Gerry. Now, Gerry was a little boy who came to see Santa Claus during my first season and he certainly showed all the signs of a budding philosopher or lawyer. Gerry was never really concerned to know his standing in Santa's book but rather what requirements were necessary to be in each book. Meaning, what exactly made up Santa's standards?

In Gerry's words: "Santa, how bad is bad? What do you consider bad and who gets the coal?"

This chapter would not be complete, though, if I didn't answer the most frequently asked of all questions. The question is one that is actually asked when I am out of the Santa Claus uniform.

Allow me to explain. It never fails that as soon as I mention to an individual that I play Santa Claus, I am asked, "Has any child ever had an accident on you?" People seem to be fascinated with this question. [Note from Santa: Actually, you're lucky, I cleaned up the phrasing of this question, and most people are a lot more graphic when they ask.] Well, the long-awaited answer is, no—at least not to my knowledge.

Rest assured, the same thought crossed my mind when I started the role. The reason why I expressed concern is because prior to my first day on the job the people in Special Events, they're the division in our store that is responsible for Santa Claus, presented me with an eight-page paper titled "A Successful Santa." The paper was created and completed to help individuals who were interested in playing the part of Santa.

The eight-page paper also made up the entire extent of my training session. One section encouraged the Santa to be "understanding and patient." It was the next line that worried me, the one that read, "Remember, the little ones are keyed-up and excited in the presence of Santa and on occasion do strange things."

It was the phrase "do strange things" that had me concerned. Fortunately, as mentioned, I'm batting a thousand, no accidents.

Though when it comes to spitting up, that's another thing.

For example, there was Stewart, a little guy no older than nine months, and his parents were determined to have a picture of him smiling on Santa's lap. The problem is you can't really make a small child like Stewart smile if he doesn't want to. They just kind of sit there like a sack of potatoes. You can bounce them on your knee and hope they let out a smile. However, this is no guarantee that they will. After all, if the child doesn't want to smile, nothing you can do will change the expression.

Stewart was just such an example of one who wasn't about to laugh or smile. The heat from the lights certainly didn't help and after five minutes, the constant bouncing was beginning to take its toll on Stewart and out came that morning's formula. Well, thank goodness for fast hands and some quick footwork by Santa's elf, for Stewart was swept off Santa's lap. I stood there with arms extended, holding Stewart out to his mother. Her response was, "Oh, that's okay."

Santa's reply, "No, that's not okay, and I think Stewart feels the same way too."

I guess you could say that for the remainder of the Santa season, I was a little gun-shy when it came to little babies. Wow, it's amazing how Similac smells even worse the second time around. And they can put a man on the moon, but they can't make baby formula smell any better!

Another question I often get asked is, "Have you ever dropped a child?"

Sadly, I must admit, I have, but not to worry, all was good in the world. Allow me to explain. It was perhaps in my second year of playing Santa and little Laura came to visit with her mom and dad. It was chilly day in Philadelphia and little Laura was dressed from head to toe in a ski suit. Santa's Helper lifted little Laura and preceded to place her on Santa's lap. Unfortunately, based on the texture of Laura's ski suit, the material made for one slippery ride. Once Santa's Helper placed Laura on Santa's lap she went sliding, right down Santa's knee and into his red bag of toys.

Mortified by what had just happened, Santa looked at Laura to see if she was hurt by the incident, but the little one treated the whole experience as an "E-ticket ride" and heralded the entire event as the funniest episode of her young life. Needless to say, Santa Claus finished the visit with Laura and her wish list while she stood safely next to him.

A lot of takeaways can come from these Q&As. One of the patterns that I've noticed during many of these exchanges is that kids have an unbelievable ability to take compliments. As adults, we are often embarrassed by any kind remark said to us by others, but kids just take comments in stride.

For example, when Santa goes to compliment a little girl on how pretty she looks that day or what a lovely name she has, I get this response ninety-nine percent of the time: "I know!"

One little girl named Courtney figured she'd get a jump on Santa's bag of compliments. I would say Courtney was no older than five when she came to visit Santa Claus. Courtney turned to Santa and before I could even get a word out she said, "Do I look pretty to you?" Santa's response was naturally, "You certainly do . . . and what a lovely name Courtney happens to be!"

"I know!"

And this, my friends, is why I took on the job for as long as I did. As they say, laughter keeps us young (even Santa)!

I COULDN'T MAKE
THIS STUFF UP

L argely, the children who have come and visited Santa Claus over the years have been pure joy. For many families, the traditional visit to see Santa is and always will be remembered as one of the more important ingredients in the life of their children. It provides the ideal setting and backdrop for every Christmas season.

However, every once in a while you get your share of children who don't feel the same sense of joy when it comes to visiting Santa Claus. They remain a perfect example as to why Santa does have a "Good" *and* a "Bad" list.

For example, I remember these two little characters like it was yesterday. They were a set of twin boys, Timmy and Jimmy, who came to see Santa many years ago. The one brother, named Timmy, seemed to be the spokesperson for the two when they both sat on Santa's lap. Timmy believed it was important for him to let Santa know about some troubling news concerning Jimmy.

Timmy turned to Santa and said, "Do you know what my brother said about you while we were in line?"

Naturally, I was expecting those tender words of affection, so Santa said, "And what would that be?"

According to Timmy, "He said that he wanted to rip your face off!"

What a little darling, I thought. I wonder if he can turn his head completely around and spit out green pea soup?

I don't understand why some children have this built-up aggression towards Santa Claus. Hey, I'm a good guy. I'm the guy with all the toys. I never did anything personally to them. But, just to be safe, I did look over my shoulder a few more times that day.

Melissa also wanted no part of Santa Claus when she came to visit. Her parents brought her and her brother Mark down to see Santa Claus one afternoon. Mark was the picture-perfect Santa visitor. Mark got right up and sat on Santa's lap, smiled from ear to ear, and then proceeded to tell me all about the wonderful toys he wanted for Christmas.

Melissa, on the other hand, ran off screaming at the first sight of Santa. Yet I was determined to get to the bottom of the problem, so I turned to Mark and asked, "You're not afraid of Santa, are you, Mark, like your sister, Melissa?"

Mark responded, "No, Santa, and Melissa's not afraid of you."

Thinking at first that fear was the obvious reason for her departure, I then asked, "Do you know why Melissa didn't want to see Santa today?'

Still smiling from ear to ear Mark simply replied, "Because she said that she hates you."

That same year, I had another little angel who also paid her respects to Santa Claus. Blake, who was no older than nine, certainly did not disguise the fact that a visit to see Santa Claus was the furthest thing from her mind. Blake had no problem sitting on Santa's lap, but based on her mannerisms she clearly preferred to be somewhere else.

To continue with the Santa legend, I gave Blake the benefit of the doubt. Santa gave her one of his traditional greetings and then I asked the standard questions.

"Now, Blake, how are you today? Haven't you grown so much since Santa Claus has seen you last? Well, what can Santa get you for Christmas?"

With each question Santa asked, Blake would not reply. The only thing Blake did was just sit there and shake her head, with this awful expression on her face. Not to fear, I continued with the now one-sided conversation. Finally after some delay, Blake replied, "I hate this! I hate this whole thing! I feel like a real idiot up here!"

Well bless her heart, I thought to myself. I knew that I didn't want her to ruin the Santa experience for any other child that may have been listening to the conversation. So I turned my next question around and asked Blake, "Don't you believe in Santa Claus?"

Blake responded immediately, "No! I don't, and I hate being up here!"

Then, I asked the question that usually calls their bluff, "Can you be absolutely sure I'm not the real Santa Claus?" It's the statement that gets them every time. It worked in Blake's case because after a brief pause she must have reconsidered all of her options and she said to Santa in a sweet little voice, "I would like a Cinderella doll and an Easy Bake Oven."

Then there was another set of twins, this one a boy and a girl. The boy, Jackson, could have demonstrated some compassion when it came to his sister Leah's wish list. Needless to say, little Leah was very eager to visit with Santa and tell him all about the toys she wanted for Christmas, in addition to this very special request. It was this special gift that her brother was finding difficult to accept with the same sense of enthusiasm.

With both kids on Santa's lap, I started my conversation first with Jackson. I then turned my attention to Leah and asked her the same question, "Is there something special you would like Santa to bring you for Christmas?"

The word "special" must have been the key word because Leah immediately became excited at the notion she could now tell Santa all about her special request.

Leah enthusiastically said, "Yes, Santa, there is something! I would like a kitty cat!"

Before Santa had a chance to utter a reply, Jackson, her twin brother, spoke up and said, "We already have a cat and it drives us all nuts!" Jackson continued with this further warning to Santa, "So you better not get her one!"

Then there was this mother one day who decided to let Santa Claus in on a little secret. Apparently, she was able to get her oldest son, Wyatt, to do some of the dirty work for her when it came to correcting the behavior of her youngest son, Jayden. The mother was hoping to use Santa Claus as well, along with his Christmas list, as the means of altering this bad behavior.

Wyatt would inform his younger brother, Jayden, that if he continued to be bad, Santa would not bring him all of the toys he wanted for Christmas. As time went by, the younger boy was not changing his devilish ways. With each bad action, his older brother was eliminating toy after toy and instructing his younger brother that this was Santa's policy.

By the time the Christmas season rolled around, the boy must have realized that Santa Claus had pretty much eliminated nearly all of his requests. So Jayden basically didn't care anymore when he came to visit Santa.

Sadly, Santa Claus was not informed by the mother concerning this plot until after the visit. Otherwise, this information would have helped before I went through my normal dissertation with the two children. Santa, naturally, asked the little boy what he would like for Christmas. Stress must have gotten the best of Jayden and he replied, "What do you care, you big piece of poop?! Haven't you taken away enough already?!"

Then there was the story of Hudson, a little boy who came to visit Santa one day with his father. Fortunately, the father informed Santa Claus, prior to the boy sitting on my lap, of a plan by his wife and Hudson's mother to correct his behavior.

Apparently, the mother kept telling Hudson, "If you aren't going to be good then I will have to call Santa Claus and tell him not to bring you any toys for Christmas!"

When Hudson did get his chance to sit on Santa's lap the first thing he said was, "Santa, ignore those phone calls from my mother. I'm better now."

Family portraits over the years have always been popular, with a few exceptions. One such portrait I seem to remember the best involved a mother, father, a seven-year-old boy, and his teenage sister. Normally, when it came to family portraits, Santa's Helpers positioned the parents behind Santa's chair with the children scattered about in front or on the lap.

Thinking this was just another family portrait, one this Santa had performed thousands of times, the parents stood behind my chair and then the Helpers positioned the younger boy on Santa's lap and then the teenage girl was just about to sit on my other leg when the brother spoke up.

The little boy turned to Santa and said, "Don't let her sit on your lap Santa, she's too heavy!"

The girl was naturally embarrassed, but after Santa reassured her, she did eventually sit. However, the boy wasn't done with his remarks. This time he turned to his sister and replied, "Santa, check out my sister, she's growing a mustache!"

At first, I felt so sorry for the teenage girl, but I was confident justice would truly be served. As soon as Santa's Helper finished taking the picture, the girl turned to her brother, smiled, and said, "Wait until we get home!"

All I can say is, I would hate to be in his shoes when they eventually got home.

A similar story occurred again the following Christmas season. Unlike the sister from the previous season, who chose to wait to settle things at home, this time after comments were made the teenage girl took immediate action. Again, Santa's Helpers were arranging the parents and the children so that a family portrait with Santa Claus could be taken.

This time, the young girl was the first to sit on Santa's lap, followed by her younger brother. As soon as the brother sat he turned to Santa and said, "Watch it Santa, your leg is about to break."

Again, unlike the first girl, this teenager was not going to wait until she got her brother home. As soon as Santa's Helpers took the picture, the girl reached over and pulled her brother's ear and said, "Come on, Scott! I've got something I want to tell you!"

I'm telling you, it wasn't pretty.

As I mentioned in one of the previous sections, at times Santa is often presented with a rather lengthy wish list.

Lillian was determined to tell Santa Claus about each and every item, but brother Billy did not have the same level of patience for his younger sister.

Lillian was concentrating on the details of her list while she proceeded to read it to Santa, "I want a Barbie doll, and a Magic Nursery doll, and a Tickle Me Elmo . . . " Lillian continued but after each request, you would hear this big sigh coming from Billy.

Lillian continued, "I want Hit Stix, I want an Etch-a-Sketch, I want . . ." Finally, by this time Billy had heard enough and it was time for him to speak up. Billy turned to his little sister, Lillian, and said, "Oh, shut up!"

The next story involves Craig and his mother, and even to this day, I'm not sure how to really title this visit with Santa. Craig was about five and he sat on Santa's lap and proceeded to tell me about all of the toys he wanted for Christmas.

The conversation continued for a few more minutes, but the entire time Craig was nervously clutching a plastic Godzilla doll. I noticed that one of Godzilla's arms had been broken off. So Santa decided to ask about his Godzilla doll, "Craig, did you know that Godzilla's arm is broken off?"

Craig replied, "It came that way when I got it."

I naturally thought to myself, *Why did they buy a toy that was defective? They should have at least returned it for a replacement Godzilla.* Obviously, there were no Elves involved in this toy-making process. It certainly would not have passed Quality Inspection.

Then Craig's mother spoke up, "Craig, tell Santa right now how you got that doll."

Craig replied, "I stole it from Nick. He's my friend."

Some friend you are!

Apparently, this too was recent news to the mother and she thought a confession by Craig to Santa Claus would help prevent further temptations for her son to steal.

Tony, on the other hand, was blunt in another way, voicing his opinion that Santa could stand a visit to the nearest Weight Watchers office. He minced no words when he blurted out, "Hey, Santa! You're fat!"

Santa sincerely thanked Tony for his "concern." Then I believe Tony thought he may have offended Santa in some way. In an effort to redeem himself Tony responded, "But that's fine, that weight looks good on you . . . don't worry if you can't fit down our chimney; we've got a big backyard. So you can park the sled out there."

Two cousins came to visit Santa one day. Both were about the same age and both were boys. The one cousin, named Landon, knew Santa Claus was all-knowing but he didn't want to take any chances when it came to the behavior and actions of his cousin Lucas, which did not sit particularly well with him.

Landon whispered to Santa, "Guess what Lucas did to me while we were in line waiting to see you?"

Expecting almost anything by this point in time, Santa responded, "What did Lucas do to you in line?"

Landon replied, "He spit in my face!"

I was dying to say at this point, "I guess it was a little 'mucus from Lucas!'" However, every Santa Claus quickly realizes one of his duties is to encourage proper behavior and good manners.

Speaking of good manners, the next story involves a little girl who could have used a lesson or two.

From what I could tell, the little girl was staying at her grandparents' house for the holidays when they came to visit Santa Claus one afternoon. Assuming this was a typical visit, Santa turned to the little girl and asked if she would like to sit on Santa's lap and tell him all about the wonderful toys she would like for Christmas.

The little girl, who we had determined was named London, responded coldly, "I find this whole thing a tremendous bore. Besides, my grandmother gets me everything I want anyway. I'm just here for a stupid picture."

Aren't you so sweet! thought Santa.

One day several seasons back, a mother and her two boys came to visit Santa Claus. All attempts by the mother had failed at keeping one child from continuing with this one troublesome habit. Apparently concerned, the mother figured wisdom from Santa may help her cause.

Her two boys made their way to Santa's lap; the oldest boy William was apparently ten years old and his younger brother, Harry, was seven years old. The mother was the first to speak, "Santa, I would like you to tell Harry that he is not permitted to play with matches."

Surprised by her words, Santa immediately echoed those same words to Harry. Then I got a little worried wondering if my beard was flammable or not.

Santa asked, "Harry, have you been playing with matches?"

This is when his older brother William spoke up, "Yep, matches, lighters . . . anything he can get his hands on!" I have to admire Harry, who didn't say a word. He just sat there, smiled, and continued to look at Santa. I, on the other hand, thought, *I know I'm going to see this kid one day on the local news.*

The story of Harry offers the perfect example as to when it is also absolutely necessary to say the right words of wisdom. Hopefully this will change the behavior and create better habits in little ones. Parents feel such advice from someone as important as Santa Claus will only help make their job that much easier.

When Santa met Samantha one year he was asked by the parents if he could express to their daughter how important it was not to kick her grandpop.

Santa turned to Samantha and said, "Remember, Samantha, it is not nice to kick Grandpa."

Her eyes told the whole story. She nodded and said, "Alright, Santa." Apparently, Samantha followed Santa's advice for about five days and the following week the parents were once again back with her to see Santa for another round of similar advice and the need not to kick Grandpop.

Another example of how Santa has been asked over the years to encourage good habits involves Bailey and her mother. As Bailey was seated on Santa's lap, her mother turned our way and said, "Santa, can you remind Bailey that she is not supposed to eat her teacher's crayons?"

As Bailey was leaving, I wondered to myself, should I ask her if all the colors taste the same and what's her favorite color?

Then there was "Little Slugger," who was affectionately named this by his father. What was consistent about Little Slugger was that his hat and jacket both had the name, "Little Slugger" sewn onto the material. Based upon my initial experience with Little Slugger, I can only imagine this little guy of four was a handful.

During Little Slugger's visit, his father quickly passed on some suggestions and advice, hoping that if Santa made mention of it to him then this may actually promote some good habits in the young lad.

So, at some point during the visit Santa Claus asked, "Little Slugger, do you know that it's important to always be good?"

His response to Santa only helped to confirm the reason for the nickname, Little Slugger, when he said, "Does this mean that I can't hit my sister Elise until after Christmas?"

A little girl named Nora, who came to visit Santa one year with her sister Mila, also had a problem with hitting. Mila, apparently, was a huge fan of the Disney film *Tangled*. I found this out after the two sat on Santa's lap and proceeded to tell him all about the great toys the two wanted for Christmas. [Note from Santa: I will be the first to admit, I love the animated feature *Tangled*. I have never gotten tired of watching it over the years with my two girls, Emma and Grace. I've always believed it is a classic in the true sense of Disney animated features.]

It was at this point that Mila turned to Santa and said, "Santa, can you tell Nora to stop hitting me with the frying pan when I'm not looking?" Nora did not deny her actions; she just sat there and had this devilish little smile on her face the whole time.

This is when the mother of the two informed Santa that Nora had watched *Tangled* one too many times. For those of you who have not seen the film, the main character Rapunzel uses a frying pan as her weapon of choice as her means of protection.

Through the years, parents and guardians have also said their share of crazy and unkind words, on occasion.

I can't tell you the number of times I've heard the expression by parents trying to soothe a crying child into seeing Santa, "Oh please sit, Grandma wants a picture!" Then there is the line that is often uttered by grandmothers who take their grandchildren down to see Santa for a picture. I hear this combination of words every year when the child begins to act up in front of the grandparent and is now reluctant to visit with Santa Claus: "Your mother never cried when I brought her down to see Santa!" Wow, what a guilt trip.

Take, for example, Sarah, a little girl no older than seven years old, when she came to visit Santa with her mother one year.

Unlike the majority of children who see Santa, Sarah did not sit on his lap. Rather, Sarah just stood alongside Santa as she read through her Christmas List. As she continued to read her list, I naturally asked Sarah if she would like to sit on Santa's lap.

It was at this point I realized why Sarah was not sitting after her mother replied, "No, Sarah, you're much too fat." I felt so sorry for little Sarah and thought about all the self-confidence issues she may experience as the years go by.

Another example of parents behaving poorly was James's mother. Apparently, James and his mother had waited in line quite a while to visit with Santa Claus. I guess the waiting, the hot lights, and the screaming children in line could get the best of anyone.

In fact, I will be the first to admit that the screaming and crying of hundreds of children can be deafening. Think about a construction site and how noisy that can get at times, now multiply that sound by ten to the second power. You can always tell the magnitude of how noisy it is getting when you look over and see Santa's Helpers popping Tylenol on the side. Speaking of crying, I always wondered, if we as adults never stopped crying when we got hungry, how loud would a typical Olive Garden waiting area be?

Sadly, from the outset, little James wanted nothing to do with Santa Claus anyway. As soon as James got a look at Santa he made his intentions clear by letting out a tremendous scream, one that to this day is floating out in space waiting to be discovered in some region of the galaxy.

However, James's mother didn't feel the same way about the situation and said quietly to her little one, "I waited in line for this man for forty-five minutes, blah, blah, blah, blah . . . and if you don't sit I'm going to beat the stew out of you."

As you can imagine, James's behavior changed rapidly.

A similar story occurred in my very first year as Santa with a little boy named Darryl. He too was accompanied by his mother on their visit to see Santa Claus.

Darryl was probably nearly ten years old and the notion of Santa Claus had started to lose its appeal. Darryl didn't cry or scream but merely said, "I don't wanna sit on no Santa Claus's lap."

In response to Darryl's comment, his mother smiled peacefully and simply replied in a quiet and calm voice, "Darryl, you better sit on this man's lap or I'm gonna break your legs."

Needless to say, Darryl perked up, smiled from ear to ear, and then Santa's Helper took the picture. As soon as the picture was taken, Darryl's facial expression went from a smile to this look of disdain.

This chapter would not be complete until I detailed the events surrounding Aubrey's visit with his grandmother. You could tell the grandmother had very good intentions when she decided to take her grandson for a visit to see Santa Claus. The little boy was, however, asleep. So, in an effort not to wake him, she gently picked up the boy out of his stroller and walked him over to see Santa.

The grandmother said, "Don't worry if he is asleep, I want the picture anyway."

I figured the little boy was just about two and there was a good chance he would sleep through the entire visit. As a family, we have often joked with our daughter Emma, who also was about two years old when she remarkably slept her way through four hurricanes our area experienced in 2004 here in Florida.

All was going well until the grandmother, as she was attempting to make the handoff of Aubrey to Santa, jolted him ever so slightly. We were hoping he would not even wake up and if he did he would just go back to sleep.

This was not the case, though, as the little boy awakened. He quickly began to focus on what was around him. I must have been his worst nightmare come true. The boy took a quick look at Santa, with eyes now bulging, screamed, and then did this Olympic-size leap off of Santa's lap and out into the main store.

The grandmother, however, was not surprised by any of this. She leaned over my way and said, "Oh, I'll be right back." Well, I thought this was the last time I was ever going to see the two of them. But I was wrong, and about fifteen minutes later I began to hear some screaming that seemed to be getting closer. Then out of the corner of my eye, I noticed the grandmother, this time without the stroller or any of her belongings, carrying her little one. It is, however, unfair to make the statement "carrying her little one." To better describe what actually occurred, the grandmother was walking slightly bent with her right hand extended down holding the ankle of her grandson, who was practically elevated and being dragged facedown across the floor. The little one was putting up a pretty good fight, with his arms extended while he pounded his fists on the marble floor.

The best analogy comes from the old *Frankenstein* movies. If you recall, there is at least one scene in the film where you see Frankenstein chasing a would-be victim. The victim is naturally running, at a sprinter's pace, and then there's Frankenstein motoring along at a snail's pace. But it never fails; Frankenstein always catches them, and in this case so did the grandmother.

FINAL MEMORABLE ENCOUNTERS WITH SANTA

The following stories involve children who will make you laugh and make you cry. These are the stories and memorable encounters between some truly unique children and Santa Claus which has helped to make the role for me so exceptional.

Take for example, Carmela, who came with her mother and grandmother for a visit to see Santa Claus one Sunday afternoon. When she was asked by Santa's Helper if she would like to sit on Santa's lap and get a picture, Carmela replied, "Nah . . . I have to get to work!"

Both shocked and amused by little Carmela's comment, Santa's Helper repeated her question as to whether she would like to sit on Santa's lap and get a picture.

This time Carmela replied, "I don't want the boss to see the picture."

By now, Santa, Santa's Helpers, and several other visitors in line who were waiting to see Santa, heard Carmela's response.

Everyone was laughing at the funny and innocent words echoed by this little girl.

Then, Carmela's mother let Santa in on a little secret. Apparently, Carmela's dad, when asked if he would like to join the group on their visit to see Santa, replied the same way. However, this was his excuse because there was a big football game on that Sunday afternoon and he didn't want to miss it. It goes to prove that you don't stand in the way of Eagles fans on game day.

Philadelphia might be known as "The City of Brotherly Love," but when it comes to Eagles football the city is notorious for its lack of affection. In fact, in 1968, Eagles fans in response to their dismal 2–12 season, once booed Santa Claus and even threw snowballs at him during a halftime show.

Well, if you were curious, Carmela did eventually sit on Santa's lap and a picture was taken, much to the satisfaction of Mom and Grandmother.

There are times when the children who visit Santa say something and you either don't hear them or just don't understand what they are actually saying. Sometimes, it is the crowd around you and the crying and screaming that is experienced in a busy Santa line. Often, you can keep the conversation going with a child by just saying, "Oh, sure," or even a cheerful nod can go a long way.

One day, I guess I learned my lesson not just to agree with whatever the child may have said, even though Santa couldn't hear or understand them. Little Stevie came to visit Santa this one particular day and said, "Hey, Santa! Do you want to see me hit myself on the head?"

Not having heard a single word that Stevie just said to me, Santa naturally replied, "Oh, sure!"

Being the good little boy that Stevie was, he then proceeded to pound his fist on the side of his head. After one or two wallops, Santa shouted, "What are you doing?"

Stevie replied, while still pounding away on his skull, "I asked, do you want to see me hit myself on the side of my head?"

This time hearing every syllable, Santa replied, "No, let's not, but maybe next year."

Then there are children like Louise, who must have figured Santa is an old guy and there is a good chance he might be a little hard of hearing. So Louise, in her loudest voice, shouted

toward Santa, "I want a Barbie doll, Shopkins, a Bratz doll, and a . . . " If I wasn't hard of hearing before, I began to feel it now.

As a department store Santa Claus, I have also experienced my share of grade school classes. It was a popular class trip for many schools for their first, second, and even third graders. In many cases, it was similar to an assembly line—one child after another would sit on Santa's lap, take a picture, and describe to Santa the contents of their wish list.

Two stories that I will always remember occurred in separate years, but they both involved the same elementary school.

The first story involved a second grader named Vincent. He was next in line to see Santa when Santa's Helper naturally went up to him. Santa's Helper did what every good Santa's Helper should do—she gathered his name so then she could secretly pass it on to Santa. This way, Santa, being the all-knowing individual that he is, would naturally know Vincent was the little's boy's name.

Then Santa's Helper decided to ask Vincent if he was going to have his picture taken with Santa.

In a concerned voice Vincent replied to Santa's Helper, "No way, baby! I'm broke! I'm flat busted!"

The second story involved Ray, a third grader, a year later. Unlike the second grader, the issue was not that Ray lacked the necessary funds to have a picture taken. It was just that he didn't quite trust everyone around him.

Ray was greeted by Santa's Helper who said, "Hello, who do we have here today to see Santa?"

The little boy insistently said, "Ray, my name is Ray, not Raymond, just Ray!"

Santa's Helper then asked, "Ray! Would you like to have a picture taken with Santa today?"

This is when Ray turned to Santa's Helper and replied, "Sure lady, but you hold the money. I don't want the guy in the chair to rip me off!"

I can only imagine Ray thought Santa was a little short of cash that day and may have been looking for an excuse to ask for his money.

On another occasion, two little girls were waiting to see Santa. When it came time for the two to sit on Santa's lap, they decided to go up separately. The first of the two girls was named Gabrielle and she was very excited to tell Santa Claus all about the toys she wanted for Christmas.

Just before Gabrielle was about to leave and make room for her friend, Santa figured he'd get a jump on the next little one in line.

"Gabrielle, is that your friend over there?" asked Santa.

"Yes, Santa, she came down with me to see you," added Gabrielle.

Naturally Santa's next question was, "And, what's your friend's name?"

Gabrielle's reply: "I forget." *Some friend you are*, I thought.

Another memorable story I like telling involves my parents. I can honestly say my parents were faithful visitors every year I was in the role of Santa Claus.

Besides, every visit usually meant lunch at some point after, and this was a good excuse for Santa to feed his reindeer. [Note from Santa: Of course, the expression, "Santa has to feed his reindeer" was code for it's time for Santa to have a lunch break.]

Naturally, a visit from my parents made for a picture-perfect moment featuring the three of us. Normally, after my parents paid their respects to Santa, they would often stand on the side, outside of Santa's house, and listen to some of the children make their way towards Santa. On this day, the next little one to see Santa was a girl named Leslie. While sitting on Santa's lap, she made an innocent comment about Santa's weight.

"Santa, you're a fat guy!"

My mother heard the comment and immediately took offense to these words about her son. She wasn't aware of the fact that such remarks are just part of the territory when playing the role of Santa. My mother was offended that someone had actually referred to her son as fat, and it took me some time to calm her down.

Speaking of the phrase, "Santa has to feed his reindeer," I remember the one year the store decided to hire a *breaker* Santa Claus. His job was basically to sit in the dressing room, in full Santa gear, and wait until I went on break. He at that point would take over Santa's chair until I got back from feeding those hungry reindeer.

Many people have asked me over the years if the store I worked at during Christmas employed more than one Santa. The answer is yes. After all, one human cannot physically, mentally, or emotionally perform the role of Santa Claus for the entire six to seven weeks that Santa makes himself visible. However, just like there is only one Mickey Mouse in the whole world, in the mind of a child, there too is only one Santa Claus.

In regards to the Santa they hired, his name was Richard, and he was a really nice guy and good for the role. However, the only problem was a matter of continuity. For example, I stand in full Santa gear about five-feet-nine-inches in height. The other Santa stood over one foot taller than I did.

So, one day, Santa's Helpers explained to the next collection of parents and children that Santa would be right out, but he had to go feed his reindeer.

One of Santa's Helpers would then escort me to the dressing room and collect the other Santa. As the other Santa was approaching the chair, the change was very noticeable, leading several of the children to scream in line, "Santa just got bigger!"

Then, I remember on one occasion, it was five o'clock on Christmas Eve. The store was just about to close for the holiday and I was pleased it was the end of another successful Santa season.

As I was approaching Santa's dressing room, a woman, along with her daughter, came running up to Santa and his Helper and asked, "Where is Santa going?"

Santa's Helper, in an effort to keep the story of Santa going, replied, "The store is closed and it is Christmas Eve so Santa is going back to the North Pole to begin his busy night!"

Knowing that Christmas was the next day, the parent then asked, "Will Santa be back again the day after Christmas?"

Obviously, she wasn't getting this whole Santa legend, and I wanted so much to reply, "Yes, Santa will be back for returns and complaints."

Another funny story involving Santa having to feed his reindeer occurred during one of my final years of playing Santa for the store. Again, one of Santa's Helpers began to accompany Santa back to his dressing room when a mother and her son approached the two of us.

The mother repeated a familiar chant, "Where's Santa going?"

Speaking on behalf of Santa, the Helper replied, "Santa is going to feed the reindeer. Santa will return soon."

So off went the mother and her little boy to either wait for Santa to return or come back at a later point. It was then that I noticed the two had stopped and the little boy made his way back to Santa and his Helper.

In a panicked and concerned voice, the boy said, "Santa is going to do what with his reindeer?"

This time Santa replied, "Santa has to go and feed the reindeer."

Now breathing a sigh of relief, the boy said, "Oh, I thought you said Santa has to go and beat his reindeer."

Terry was a little girl about nine years old when she came to visit Santa a few seasons ago along with her mother. Terry faced a dilemma that she was hoping Santa could help solve. Apparently, Terry's mother unfortunately had to work on Christmas Day, and she naturally wanted her mother home for the holidays.

The conversation went something like this: "Hello, Terry, have you come to visit Santa and tell him about all of the wonderful toys you would like him to bring you for Christmas?"

Hoping that Santa could use his influence Terry replied, "Yes, Santa, but before I begin could you see what you can do about talking to Mommy's boss and see if he can give her Christmas Day off?"

Speaking of Christmas Day, Channel came to visit one year and was just a little confused about this whole Christmas ritual. Channel knew that she wanted one item in particular for

Christmas; she just wasn't sure when the item was supposed to show up.

Channel was very pleasant and was enjoying her visit with Santa on that day.

Santa turned to Channel and asked, "What can Santa get you for Christmas?"

In a soft voice, Channel replied, "I want a bouncy ball."

Santa replied, "Wow, you want a bouncy ball; did you want any certain color?"

"I want a red one," said Channel excitedly.

"Channel, would you like anything else for Christmas from Santa?"

"No, that's it!" replied Channel. We chatted for a few more minutes. I thanked Channel for coming to visit Santa, and then she was on her way.

About an hour or two later, all of a sudden, Channel appeared yet again. This time, Channel looked a little concerned and she proceeded to look into Santa's house and shout my way, "Where's my bouncy ball?"

Channel might have been cute, but she just didn't have the whole Christmas process down yet.

The next two stories involve a couple of "Doubting Thomases," or in other words non-believers. Over the years I have certainly gotten my share of children who have questioned the authenticity of me as Santa or even the concept behind Santa himself. So when I would come across a non-believer or doubter who would make a statement such as "You're not Santa Claus!", my reply back would always be, "Can you be absolutely sure I'm not the real Santa Claus?"

Not wanting to tempt fate at this point, the child usually retreated from the accusation, fearing a possible wrath by the one and only Santa. However, Jeffrey needed a little more convincing.

Santa asked Jeffrey the age-old question, "What can Santa get you for Christmas?"

Then Jeffrey blurted out that all too familiar statement, "You're not Santa Claus!"

Santa's reply back to Jeffrey: "Can you be absolutely sure I'm not the real Santa Claus?"

Then a long pause from Jeffrey before he finally spoke, "If you are the real Santa Claus, then I want to see some identification. Do you have a driver's license?"

From what I can remember, I believe I answered Jeffrey's question this way, "Santa left it back in his sled."

The second "Doubting Thomas" was Sean, and he too wanted to see some identification. Sean was introduced to Santa by one of Santa's Helpers. Santa greeted Sean and then proceeded to ask Sean what he would like for Christmas. Then Sean made the statement, which in some ways truly hurts all of those caring individuals out there who play the role of Santa Claus, "You're not Santa Claus!"

Once again, Santa replied, "Can you be absolutely positive that I'm not the real Santa Claus?"

Conceding slightly, Sean replied, "Okay . . . if you are the real Santa Claus, take off your white glove and let me see your hands."

What my hand had to do with it, I haven't a clue. But to appease Sean, I did take off my one glove. Sean wasn't finished with Santa yet, so he made another request, "And if you are, who you say you are, then I want you to leave a picture of yourself behind when you visit our house on Christmas Eve."

Often the role of Santa Claus is not always filled with a sugar-coated pathway. At times, you are faced with many sad stories from children who visit Santa. If you think about Santa in the hierarchy of a small child's life, he's a pretty important guy. The little ones look up to Santa in an almost saintlike manner. Santa in some cases can almost represent for a child, their last hope.

One such story involved Crystal, a little girl no older than four. Crystal sat up on Santa's lap and instead of asking for some toys for Christmas, she said sadly, "Santa, they said my daddy may not be coming home from the hospital, can you make him better?"

From what I could tell from Crystal's grandmother, her father had a massive heart attack at work and the doctors were not promising much hope for his recovery. What do you say to a child that makes this type of request? What you want to do is give her a big hug and tell her that everything is going to be alright because you're Santa Claus.

However, reality sets in and you come to the realization that miracles like those don't happen overnight. It is moments like this when you wish you were truly Santa Claus.

Honestly, all you can do is reply, "Santa will say a prayer for your daddy."

Most of the time, this will soothe the child's spirits, but you know deep down that they were wishing for more.

Then there are times that it seems unfair to refer to the children as children, considering how mature they really are. Reality is often unfair to the children when it robs them of their childhood. Tucker asked Santa for one request, "Can you help my father get his life back in order?"

I'm not sure of all the particulars surrounding this child, but again all I could say in reply was, "Santa will say a prayer for your daddy."

Another uncomfortable situation you are faced with at times while playing the role of Santa Claus is when children find themselves in the middle of a recent divorce. Take for instance, Donny, a five-year-old that found himself right in the middle of a custody battle. It hurts you when a child says, "My mommy and daddy don't live together anymore, and can you get my daddy back?"

The downtown Philadelphia area where I played the role of Santa Claus for the department store really symbolized a melting pot for the children I saw over the years. Some were very rich and well-to-do, while others you could tell came from families who were barely making it.

Some of the sweetest children this Santa had encountered over the years were those children who didn't ask for many things for themselves at all for Christmas. Their Christmas wishes were generally for their mommy or daddy or another family member. They might ask for a new pair of slippers for their mommy and her tired feet or a pair of warm gloves for their daddy, who had to be outside in the freezing weather.

During the Christmas of 1990, as you might recall, the United States was sending troops to help solidify positions in and around the country of Kuwait. The United States was for all intents and purposes bracing for all-out war on Iraq. That period of time was a nerve-wracking one for most Americans as well as for children. One day, I too felt the effects of this action taken by the country. It involved Adrien, a little boy whose father was just sent to Saudi Arabia as a pilot for the 193rd Special Operations Group. Well, to make a long story short, Adrien was concerned that Santa Claus during his traditional Christmas Eve journey may run into some unfriendly fire over the Middle East.

Adrien asked, "Santa, do you think it is going to be too dangerous for you to fly over Iraq?"

To ease Adrien's worries Santa said, "Don't worry about Santa. He represents everything good in the world and again you don't have to worry."

He then asked Santa, "That's great and when you do go, can you deliver this letter to my daddy while you're over there?" Adrien handed me a sealed envelope marked "Daddy."

This book would not be complete without telling you the story of Kembry. Personally, this story happens to be one of my favorites.

Kembry was a little boy no older than five, who came for a visit to see Santa Claus in one of my final seasons playing the role for the department store. Kembry was accompanied by his father and the two were apparently tourists visiting family members in the area.

The father was the first to speak. "Kembry, tell Santa where you are from."

Already sitting comfortably on Santa's lap, Kembry replied, "We're from St. Catharines."

Fortunately, Santa was familiar with his geography and replied, "St. Catharines, that's in Ontario."

Excited that Santa knew his hometown, Kembry replied back, "That's right!"

However, at the outset Kembry wasn't completely sure if Santa knew on the map where St. Catharines was. So Kembry brought with him a little inflatable globe and began to point to where he and his father lived. After some convincing, Santa was able to assure Kembry that because Canada was so close to the North Pole, it naturally was one of Santa's first stops on Christmas Eve.

Now it was down to business, "Kembry, is there anything you would like Santa to bring you for Christmas?"

Without hesitation Kembry replied, "I want a violin, a piano, a cello . . ."

Kembry proceeded to give Santa a whole laundry list of requests that he wanted for Christmas, and every single one of the items was a musical instrument. When Santa does encounter a rather long list, I will often repeat a request to show interest and keep the conversation rolling.

For instance, in Kembry's case Santa said, "Oh, you want a cello."

Kembry thought this repeating by Santa meant that he didn't understand the request.

So, when Santa said, "Oh, a cello," Kembry replied, "You know what a cello is Santa Claus? It's like a big violin!"

Well, I guess Kembry made his point clear. Kembry continued with his requests after setting Santa straight. Still, the only items he was asking for were more musical instruments.

After Kembry finished, Santa naturally asked the logical question, "Kembry, you must be a musician."

However, the word "musician" must not have been part of Kembry's vocabulary yet because he replied, "No, I'm not a musician; I'm a little boy!"

I'll leave you with one final story, which involves my own three children. For more than a decade, I was extremely fortunate to have my own children visit me when I played the role of Santa Claus for the cruise line.

I remember they came to visit Santa with their traditional wish list in hand and of course a picture I helped craft with them the night before. Again, little did they know that they would visit me, their dad, as Santa.

Needless to say, it was one of my proudest moments each year. However, I remember one year, my oldest daughter Emma, who was no older than six at the time of this particular visit, commented at the dinner table later that night to me and my wife, "Santa sounds like daddy!"

Shocked at what we heard, I knew at the time that I needed to keep the magic alive, so my response went something like this, "Of course he does, and Santa will always sound like someone you love! He might sound like your grandfather, a special uncle, or even your mother!"

That was all Emma needed to hear to ensure that the magic lived on!

ACKNOWLEDGMENTS

I would like to take this opportunity to thank my friends and family for their love and support. I also want to thank my editor, Julie Ganz, and the team at Skyhorse Publishing for helping to spread a little Santa magic by bringing this book into reality.

I especially want to thank my version of Mrs. Claus—my wife, Susan—along with my three Helpers—my children Matthew, Emma, and Grace.

ABOUT THE AUTHOR

Kevin Neary has coauthored *Disney He Said—She Said* (2018), *The Hidden Mickeys of Walt Disney World* (2016), and *Maps of the Disney Parks: Charting 60 Years from California to Shanghai* (2016) with his wife Susan, and four Disney trivia books (1992–2000) with Dave Smith for The Walt Disney Company. In addition, he has written and published two baseball books: *Major League Dads: Baseball's Best Players Reflect on the Fathers Who Inspired Them to Love the Game* (2012) and *Closer: Major League Players Reveal the Inside Pitch on Saving the Game* (2013) for Running Press. Kevin has also written: *715: Reflections of Hammerin' Hank & the Home Run that Made History* (2015) for Skyhorse Publishing.

WISH LIST

....

....

....

....

....

....

....

....

....

....

....

WISH LIST

....

....

....

....

....

....

....

....

....

....

....

....

WISH LIST

....

....

....

....

....

....

....

....

....

....

....

WISH LIST

WISH LIST

••

••

••

••

••

••

••

••

••

••

••

••

WISH LIST

....

....

....

....

....

....

....

....

....

....

....

....

WISH LIST

....

....

....

....

....

....

....

....

....

....

....

WISH LIST

WISH LIST

· ·

· ·

· ·

· ·

· ·

· ·

· ·

· ·

· ·

· ·

· ·

· ·

WISH LIST

WISH LIST

....

....

....

....

....

....

....

....

....

....

....